Mystic Saints Of India: 7

Meera Bai

B. K. CHATURVEDI

Series Editor : (Dr.) Mahendra

BOOKS FOR ALL
Delhi-110052

Distributed by
D. K. Publishers Distributors Pvt. Ltd.
24, Ansari Road, Darya Ganj,
New Delhi-110 002
Phs. : 327 8368, 326 1465, 327 8584
Fax : 326 4368
E-mail : dkpd@del3.vsnl.net.in
Web site:www.dkpd.com.

First Published : 2002

ISBN 81-7386-245-1(Meera Bai)
ISBN 81-7386-231-1 (Series)

Published by :
Books For All
(an imprint of Low Price Publications)
A-6, Nimri Commercial Centre,
Near Ashok Vihar Phase-IV, Delhi-110 052
Ph. : 740 1672, 745 2453
E-mail : Ipp@nde.vsnl.net.in
Web site:www.Ippindia.com.

Printed at
D. K. Fine Art Press Pvt. Ltd.
Delhi-110052 Ph. 745 2451

Printed in India

PREFACE

Meera is perhaps the lone saint-poetess of India, particularly of the Hindi belt. Yet her renown knows no bounds. It is to pay our homage to this lyricist of incomparable simplicity and charm on her 6th centenary that this work has been undertaken. The emphasis, in general, has been revealing her life through her verses since no authentic biography on her is available either in Hindi or in English or even in the regional languages, barring few apocryphal anecdotes. Hence, the assiduous selection of her 36 'padas' which convey the essence of her style of devotion, apart from also giving details about her personal life, though obliquely are presented here. The translation of her verses has been liberally punctuated with foot-notes to help the reader reach to the very root of the meaning. The authenticity of the period has also been cross-checked with available historical records. The geographical locations of the spots and places associated with her have been given in a separate chapter to help the readers willing to do further research in the matter.

So, the work is in your hands, dear readers! We hope that you would lovingly join this attempt of ours to learn more and more about this unique saint-poetess of India and this way offer a tribute to her.

Lastly, the author expresses his gratitudes to Mittal Brothers of 'Books For All' for giving him liberal help and support in preparing this book.

B.K.CHATURVEDI

SERIES' EDITOR'S NOTE

In 1963, Dr. Radhakrishnan, the President of India, declared in Bombay, "The time has come for all countries to work towards making the world a single home for Humanity.....Economics, Politics and transport have done their jobs. But we have to do as to give a soul to the world which has found a body, you can give it if you are truly Indian." We Indians are proud to have so many mystic saints who contributed to the upliftment of humanity.

In Indian thought, there are two modes in which we acquire knowledge: Argument and Experiment. Both these modes, together with experience play an important role in the development of mankind. Saints of India, through their arguments, tried to communicate their experiences to human beings. This represents an adventure in thinking.

This series, it is hoped, will enable the reader, eastern or western, to understand and appreciate currents of Indian thought by depicting the life and writings of different saints. We have tried to portray the true picture of Indian culture. I am really thankful to all those who have helped in preparing and publishing these books, as they will not only propagate the ideas of Indian saints, but also help in making mankind a better race.

Our world becomes wider, our imagination richer and our life more colourful and more zestful as a result of our companionship with these saints, who are the travellers of the spirit and the pioneers of thought.

25.7.01 **(DR.) MAHENDRA**

CONTENTS

"The bardy's sublime
Whose distant footsteps echo
Through The Corridors of Time"

—Longfellow

1

Meera: A Unique Saint-Poetess of Northern India

Although India is believed to be a favourite nursery that has mystic saints owing to its general psyche nurtured rooted in spiritualism, Meera stands as a unique product of this nursery, due to many reasons. First of all, despite the traditional dominance of orthodoxy in Medieval India when she hit the mystic firmament of India, she was a rebel. She violated the norms of the most traditional and respected dynasty of that time: the Mewar Dynasty. This dynasty is believed to be the crown jewel of the Hindu raj-vansha (royal families) with many renowned rulers like Rana Kumbha, Rana Sanga, to Rana Pratap radiating their glories from Chittorgarh, the Capital of Mewar. Great believers in the "Parda System" in which the ladies of the household were to be kept as aloof from the common people as to make them aspire to become asooryam-prishya' (untouched even by the sun-rays), these rulers of Mewar and their chieftains—as bigoted as their masters—received a great shock, enough to shake the very foundations of their orthodox mindset when they heard that one of the widows of the royal household was intermingling with the peripatetic holy men, throwing taboos to wind. Meera didn't show only as much courage as to declare her love for someone she was not legally wedded to, but she also neglected her formally wedded husband to the great chagrin of the entire society of the time. And why did she do so? How an uneducated and unexposed woman could take such a 'bold' step? She did not have any extra marital relation; she was pious to the core. But she had the strength of her guileless and self-less devotion for her chosen lord, Shree Krishna. To a modern mind her doing this might appear inexplicable, and one might question the sanity of such a woman. But this is the strength of her divine love. It is the pristine purity of her love for God which provided her courage. She is the only woman that showed her love for someone so ethereal could defy all forms of the accepted social order. She rose much higher than all caste and creed considerations to see the whole world permeated by only one existence that of Lord Krishna!

Although she was the lone woman to take such a drastic route, this had been the trend of that period during the Middle ages when oppressed by alien rulers the people sought succour in divine worship. This trend has been given a specific name called the 'Bhakti Movement', which rose due to various conditions of the period. Unlike the earlier invaders who attacked and eventually stayed in India only, the Muslim invaders preserved their separate entity on account of a feeling of superiority to the natives as well as their adherence to Islam with a tenacity and enthusiasm unknown in India. But the contact between the Muslims and Hindus produced an intermingling of the two faiths, that removed many oddities in the character of both. With the settlement of Muslims in India, a new spirit, the oneness of God, appeared to appeal to the polytheistic Hindus. Thus was born the Bhakti Movement which represented in its essence the spirit of judiçious synthesis of Hinduism and Islam.

The first exponent of this movement was Ramanuja who preached the unity of God (under the cult of Vaishnavism) in the 11th century in South India. In the north emerged many saints and poets, the believers in this synthesis, like Ramananda, Kabir, Nanak and Dadu etc. Meera was a product of this movement but she carried the stamp of her distinct style. She never preached any cult worship nor indulged in difficult metaphysical analyses. Her message was simple: total submergence of one's identity in that of the chosen deity. For her God didn't remain an impersonal existence. She deemed him as her beloved who had particular traits and style, who responded to his devotee's overtures in his typical divine manner. Meera would bathe him and feed him as though he was a human being. In fact, personification of her chosen lord owing to her intense feeling of love borders partially on insanity. But that sort of empathy appears unique in her case. The descriptions to convey her feeling are the gems of lyrical poetry of the Medieval Ages. It is due to her this intensity of devotion, despite her running counter to the accepted norms of her times, that she transcended her age and came to be accepted as something novel to the Indian tradition of Bhakti. Although Tulsidas's devotion to Rama and Surdasa's devotion to Krishna were no less intense but what distinguishes

Meera's poetry is her personal and 'unborrowed' experience. She felt as though she was herself Lord Krishna's bride and she had no need to imagine the agony of Radha to describe her feelings. All her 'padas' (verses as they are called) convey so intense a feeling that they instantly develop a rapport with the reader. She conveyed as she felt without incurring any 'transmission loss'. Since she was barely literate (even that is claimed to be doubtful), she never minces her words and reproduced verbatim her experience in a typical form. Her poetry is that of feeling and her message is guileless and unadulterated love. Neither did she preach a religion like Nanak did, nor like Kabir did she reform a degenerating society. She transcends all these mundane considerations and stands peerless as a lyrical poetess of love.

And what was unique in her character was the fact that the more she was opposed, the greater intensity she developed to pursue her chosen path. Under the rule of Mewar, particularly under her brother-in-law Vikramaditya's reign, she was subjected to a variety of tortures; she was made to drink poison, lie on thorn laden-bed and even an attempt was made to let her die of snake-bite. But undaunted, and helped by her 'Divine Companion', she kept on moving on her path of unswerving devotion to eventually win a niche in the firmament of India's renowned saints cum poets. She herself appears a personification of a 'Jogin' i.e. a female totally lost in her beloved's love. She appears to be a natural poetess. She chose the words irrespective of their root or origin—even if they were not much cultured for their use in poetry. It is their pristine rawness that hits the readers with its full impact as is the case with Kabir's dohas. She wrote what she felt. Of course there is a difference as to which language she wrote in: Rajasthani, Gujarati or archaic medieval Hindi, but the fact is that she wrote in the language unadulterated by any linguistic considerations. Hers is the language of a love-lorn heart: full of pathos, intensity and feeling. Although the research scholars claim that she had composed as many as seven to eight books of poetry, including '*Narasi ji ko Mehra*', except her loose 'padas' nothing is available now. It is from these collections that these 'Padas' or 'Bhajanas' composed by Meera have been culled and included in this book. While no claim about their authenticity can be made apart from the general form and contents, an attempt has been made to choose those verses that reveal about her biography as well. Since there is no authentic detail about her life, barring a few anecdotes and popular legends available, in the words of T.S Eliot we can claim that 'we have evoked her biography from the lines of her poems.' Let alone her life, even her death is still a mystery. She is said to have dissolved her existence and was finally absorbed in a stone idol of Lord Krishna! Ironically, despite her 'Bhajanas' and 'Padas' that have regaled the readers for now more than half a millennium, nothing is authentically known about her save what is revealed by her verses. She was born in 1506 A D and the country on the very basis is gearing up to celebrate her advent's 6th centenary.

However, despite the lack of details, Meera's popularity has never waned. Her 'bhajanas' have always remained a part of the country's rich heritage. No North

Indian musician thinks his or herself as perfect if his or her repertoire doesn't contain a few chosen verses of Meera. Often she is compared with Vidaal of South but the comparisons is quite odd since compare the persons and not the circumstances they had lived in. Any lesser being in Meera's place would have succumbed to tortures and agonies she was subjected to but not Meera. Her grit and determination kept on growing more strong as the opposition to her fetter-free living style. For, in her love for Lord Krishna she cared not for any obstructions or impediments; perhaps they were too puny to merit her attention.

What charms Meera's 'Bhajanas' apart from their direct heart to heart content, is their music. It is because they were not only composed by them but she herself used to sing before her Lord's image. That is why it was considered proper to include the text, their Romanised version and translation in the second part of the book, so that going through the text the readers could also enjoy the lyricism of the verses. Translations have been given them derive their full meaning. This way it could be claimed as a comprehensive volume on Meera.

2

Her Birth and Early Years

Rajasthan, the north-west bordering state of India, is renowned for its legends of bravery and chivalry all over the world, thanks to the book authored by Col. Todd. It has been a famous nursery of warriors who gladly sacrificed their life for the sake of their mother land. This is the land of Gora and Badal, of Rana Pratap and Rana Sanga, of Padmini and Panna. Apart from bravery being ingrained in their very blood, there have also emerged famous saints and seers who with their compositions inspired the people in love and devotion as well. They taught the people how to love their mother land and their chosen deity with as much faith and devotion as is very rare.

It was in the kingly state of Jodhpur that there ruled the dynasty of Rathods who claim their descent from Jaichand of Kannauj. There is no definite record about it but it is generally believed that Seeha Ji had established this stronghold of Rathods in Marwar. His descendant was Rao Jodha Ji who established the city of Jodhpur. Rao Jodha's fourth son was Rao Dooda Ji who is believed to be the origin of the sub-branch of the Rathods called Meratiya, since they settled themselves in a small place called Merata.

Rao Dooda Ji had two queens who produced five sons and one daughter for the Rao. His fourth son's name was Ratna Singh. Meera was the daughter of Ratna Singh. Meera's mother was a Tankali Rajpoot and her name was Kusum Kunwar.

According to the local legends Meera's mother died when she was only a small child. In order to provide the motherless daughter good care and affection, Rao Dooda called her to Merata, his stronghold to look after her. Meera began to live with her grand parents in Merata city.

Although there is no authentic record to pin-point Meera's date of birth, according to various legends and anecdotes she was born on Ist lunar date of the bright fortnight of the month of Shrawan in Samvat 1561 which corresponds to 1505 A.D.

Meera was a born devotee to God. Her father's (Ratna Singh's) elder brother Veeramdev was a well-known devotee. He is said to have composed many verses singing the glories of God, but they are not available, barring a few scattered references of them in Rajasthani folk songs. However, his praise by the contemporary saints is still found in certain devotional compositions.

Even Meera's grandfather, Dooda Ji was also a very pious and religious person. He was a liberal Vaishnava who had the temple of Devi 'Chaterbhuja' constructed in Merata.

Owing to this atmosphere at home, Meera naturally developed a religious bent of mind. From a very tender age she had started keeping fasts and participating in various religious festivals with a natural gusto.

There is an interesting legend about her developing so overpowering love for Lord Krishna.

When she was very young, one day she was sitting with her mother on the roof-terrace of the palace. Suddenly she heard the roar of the blaring trumpets and pounding of the drums accompanying a procession moving amidst the portable lights. Suddenly all her cousins and the maid servants rushed to the edge of the roof terrace to watch the commotion down below on the road. Meera being a small child couldn't understand the cause of their enthusiasm. She asked her mother, "Ma! What are they watching with so much of enthusiasm? Why these lights and the noise?"

"Beti", replied the mother, "There is a *barat* (marriage procession) going down there. They all have gone to watch it."

"But what is a *barat*, Ma?" the curious girl persisted.

"*Barat* is the conglomeration of the people from the groom-side. They come here to get a bride for their groom. They all come with much pomp and show as it is a happy occasion when a wedding takes place. "Having allowed the information to sink in for a few moments, the daughter again asked.

"And who is the groom?"

Now, the mother was somewhat annoyed and said in a peevish tone: "Groom is the boy who comes to wed his bride through a nuptial ceremony. Now you don't pester me with your questions as I have to do my evening worship." The mother left but the daughter continued to trail her mother. While the mother was cleaning the small idol of Lord Krishna and preparing herself for the worship, the daughter (Meera) again asked:" Who is my groom?" The annoyed mother then pushed the idol of Lord Krishna down into her daughter's hands and said:" He is your groom, now keep quiet."

While the mother busied herself with the evening worship, Meera kept on looking at the idol with great enthusiasm, thinking:" How comely are his eyes and how captivating is his form.' And look at the nose and the ears—looking so beautiful with the crocodile shaped earings."

When mother asked for the idol, Meera refused to part with it. "This is my groom! I wont' give him to you" with her juvenile delinquency. At last she agreed when mother said," All right. You take your 'groom' to the throne made here and worship as I say."

Since then it became a ritual. Everyday it was Meera only who started doing the worship of the 'Thakur Ji' under her mother's guidance. How great was Lord Krishna's divine influence over Meera can be judged by Meera's these lines which she penned much later. Mentally she had accepted Lord Krishna as her groom and would imagine all kinds of dalliance, while playing the bride's role and Lord Krishna that of the groom. She writes:

"Mayee ree mhane supane main parana gaye gopal!
Raat peeri chunar paharee mehndee paan rasal!
Kayeen karan aur sanga bhanwar mhane jag janjal!
Meera Prabhu Giridharan Lal soon, karee sagayee hal!

[O Mother! In dream I chose Gopal as my groom . In the night I donned the yellow apparel, put henna to make my hands and feet red. I ate a betel-leaf (to redden my lips). He is the ideal choice for me since the rest of the world appears to be only giving me a headache. So, Meera has been recently bethroted to him who had mounted the hill (of Goverdhan) upon his finger].

This way mentally she accepted Krishna as her groom and husband. Whatever she learnt about a wife should do, she practised doing everything when in her imagination she reached near the groom. Her worship and love for Krishna continued to grew intense more and more each day.

Meanwhile, her mother expired. That was a great blow for Meera because she lost that protection under which she could have continued her loveful dalliance with her chosen groom. Now she was also becoming nubile-according to standard prevalent then, although she was hardly 12. Since her mother was no more her father was particularly worried. Knowing something about his daughter, he wanted to discharge his responsibility as soon as possible.

He sent his barber (as was the practice that time) with the marriage proposal to every princely house. After much searching and scrutiny, Ratna Singh concentrated Rana Sangha's second son Bhojraja. He was to be Meera's groom in the mortal realm.

3

Marriage and Tribulations

Meera's marriage to Rana Sangha's son Bhojraj was settled out of many political and diplomatic considerations. Meera's father was a mere feudal lord of only 12 villages whereas Rana Sangha was the ruler renowned all over North India as a very brave and chivalrous king of India's most esteemed dynasty that traced its descent right from Lord Rana's solar dynasty of mythological era. Apart from the reason that Meera was an extremely charming girl who could have added to the pride of any princely state, she belonged to the Rathod branch of the brave Rajpoots (race of princes) which was also an esteemed martial race. The third reason was mainly of political concern. Notwithstanding Rana Sangha being a renowned ruler his house was a divided lot, fraught with many intrigues and dissensions. The Rana had seven sons: Pooranmalla, Bhojraj, Parvat Singh, Ratna Singh, Vikramaditya, Krishna Singh and the youngest Udaya Singh (the father of redoubtable Rana Pratap). The mothers of Udaya Singh and Vikramaditya, Rani Karmeti, and the mother of Ratna Singh, Dhanabai, were sworn enemies of each other. They always indulged in vile intrigues to let the other down. As far as the Rana was concerned, no doubt he had been hailed as the 'Arch Crown of the Hindus'. Yet he, nevertheless, lacked the tact and diplomatic acumen to maintain that high a status. He was very brave and fearless no doubt, but states cannot be run merely on the strength of individual bravery. At that time the Rathods were Mewar's enemy arch. The Rana (Rana Sangha) thought that in having relations by marriage with the Rathods he would be killing two birds with one stone: getting a good bride for his son and having family relations with one of the strongest clans of the Rajpoots and turning them into Mewar's well-wishers.

Since the country had started witnessing invasions from the Muslim rulers, particularly from the north-west side, this reunion between the two strongest and most reputed clans of the Rajpoots was bound to prove beneficial for the entire Hindu race.

Moreover, Rao Dooda ji had his large number of followers owing to his diplomatic skill, far sight as well as his personal valour. Also, his image of being a god-fearing, honest and brave person had weighed heavily on the Mewar ruler, in Rana Sangha's estimation.

And so the marriage was solemnised with great pomp and show. After Meera's marriage with the Rana's son Bhojraj, the Rathods kept on supporting the Sisodias of Mewar.

While everyone was greatly pleased and gratified with this marriage, Meera herself was the lone exception. She was shedding tears of blood, as it were. The swelling tide of tears never stopped even for a moment. As the ceremonial circumambulations around the fire were over, signifying the completion of the ceremony, she rushed to her "Sanwalia' (the Dark One i.e. to her chosen Lord Krishna's idol) and silently registered her grievances. She never wanted to marry the second time! Wasn't she already married to Krishna? Every grain of her body appeared to register its protest against this forced marriage. But she was helpless and couldn't have refused the marriage. But how could she prove that she was already married? To whom? To a mere idol? Or to an only emotional existence whom she couldn't exhibit? Nevertheless she had to accept the grim reality that she was to be married to Bhojraj.

The time for her formal separation from her parent's family called Vidaa was fast approaching. At last she summoned the courage to say to her father: "Please allow me to carry this idol of Sanwalia!" The bemused father readily accepted the demand. Who would object to her carrying a mere idol with her? Little did he realise that the idol was the centre of life for his 12 year old Meera.

Thus, Meera left Merata with her Giridhara pressed to her bosom. She reached the most famous citadel of warriors, Chittorgarh, renowned as the most formidable fort in entire Rajasthan. She was now the youngest bride of the royal house of Chittorgarh which put her under many a restriction.

But perhaps Meera was not destined to enjoy the nuptial bliss of the mortal kind. While she was still in her teens her husband expired. Although not much is known as to how Bhojraj died, local legends claim that perhaps snake-bite was the cause.

Meera had become a widow in the prime of her youth. Now, being a widow is the greatest stigma for a woman in the traditional Hindu households. Since she has to live under the fetter of innumerable restrictions in the medieval times, a cruel practice was popularised for the sake of preserving the woman's purity. They evolved a system called 'Sati-Pratha'. In this the widowed woman had to burn herself to death along with her dead husband's body. It was downright an inhuman system whose traces are still found at the threshold of the 21st century, but at that time it was the most encouraged practice.

It is believed that the senior members of the royal household including Rana Sangha might have suggested her following the celebrated practice, Meera who deemed herself 'ever wedded to her Lord Sanwalia' refused to bow before their desire. She might have become widow for the mortal world, in her ethereal world, she was still with her beloved husband. Perhaps that was the beginning of the troubles for her. But, undaunted, she became more and more drawn towards her 'Sanwalia' caring two hoots to all her mortal duties. In fact, she was hardly perturbed by her husband Bhojraj's death. In none of her verses she ever expressed any thought about him; as if he never existed for her. Though physically she might have been forced to call Bhojraj her husband yet she never considered herself to be his wife. Since her soul was drenched in the love of her 'Sanwalia', for her any mortal relation was of the least consequence.

We have our scriptures always teaching us that all the mortal bonds are transitory; they are by nature impermanent because our physical self is but an illusion. True is only that relationship which binds your soul to God. Since Meera's soul was bound with that of 'Sanwalia', the permanent, ever-present existence with which the whole universe is ever instinct, why should she have given a thought to any relation which is intrinsically impermanent? Right from day one of her marriage, her mind never accepted any existence other than her Beloved Lord. Of course this might have created for her some troubles in Chittorgarh but what significance did her mortal marriage have is clear by her never even referring about it in her poems. Although she did refer about the tortures that the later Rana, Vikramaditya tried to inflict upon her, as far as her relations with her mortal husband are concerned we draw a total blank. Much later she was to convey her with total indifference to him when she sang:

"Mere to Giridhara Gopal.
doosaro no koyee
Jake sir mor-mukat
merau pati soyee'

[None except Giridhara Gopal is my beloved; he alone is my husband who holds a peacock-feather crown upon his head].

Now, with that mortal bond broken, Meera felt, in a sense, relieved. With this fetter gone she was now totally devoted to her divine love for Lord Krishna.

In the initial years of her widowhood, she was supported by Rana Sangha who was a kind hearted father-in-law. He thought Meera's religious fervour was a natural cover to hide her sorrow. It is a normal psychology. We still witness people becoming more devoted to God when they lose someone near and dear to them. With this thought the Rana remained considerate to his son's widow. Moreover, till that time Meera's father, Ratna Singh Rathod, was also alive. He would also keep on extending his protective hand upon his young and recently widowed daughter.

But things worsened when Rana Sangha was killed in the famous battle against the Mughal invader Babur. It is a well known event of Medieval history which established Babur in India and the Mughal era began with Babur consolidating his position after this war.

But this war proved highly unfortunate for Meera. Her father, Ratna Singh, who was an able lieutenant of Rana Sangha, was also killed in this battle. The Rana was also badly wounded and, later on, he succumbed to his injuries. The death of father-in-law and father started the most unfortunate phase in Meera's life. With both the Rana's gone, a war of succession began among his surviving sons. The palace intrigues began to be plotted and no one could rely on the other. Unfortunately, none of the late Rana's sons was competent enough to hold the throne for long. Eventually Vikramaditya, the fifth son managed to grab the throne. Now, he was a wicked person. He had no consideration for his elder brother's widow who, according to him, was ruining the family prestige.

Although Meera felt distressed by these sudden developments in the royal household, she began to find more and more solace in singing songs composed by her in the love of her beloved 'Sanwalia'. She began to spend more and more time in the company of Sadhus and holy persons. Everyday she would visit a temple and return with a noble holyman talking to her about her real Beloved. She threw all the etiquettes that the royal ladies were expected to follow, to winds. Should she listen about the arrival of some renowned saint, breaking all norms of decorum she would herself go to welcome and honour him. Her apparently gay-cavillier manners began to hurt the traditional eye of the most noble Hindu family. The seniors of the family started questioning her attitude. She became subjected to all sorts of innuendoes which included those that attempted to slurring her character also. What added fuel to fire was Meera's extreme beauty and youth. She was still very young. Her beauty was enough to captivate even the ascetics and hermits. And beauty, widowhood and such unfettered, totally free life style always ill go together. Even in the beginning of the 21st century such ladies would be looked down upon with unconcealed derogation, let alone Meera in the Medieval ages. With the result, without realising the truth in Meera's heart, the society started painting her as a woman of loose moral behaviour. The upholder of the social norms never minded Meera doling out alms to the needy holymen, devoting large amounts for the construction of temples but certainly they objected to her singing songs with strangers of unknown descent and even dancing amidst them. This certainly damaged the reputation of the royal household of Chittorgarh!

But Meera was hardly concerned with all these secular considerations since she was much above them, ever in the company of her beloved Lord Krishna. She never cared for the innuendoes and aspersions obliquely hurled at her.

In fact, immediately after Rana's death, his son Ratna Singh ascended to the throne. But the vile palace intrigues didn't allow this Rana, Ratna Singh, to survive for long. He was not as harsh on Meera and treated her with due honour. But the mutual feuds among the various queens ensured his death, almost in less than a decade to Rana Sangha's death. Since Ratan Singh's wife was also a Rathod girl, she provided a natural protection to Meera through exercising her influence upon her son who was also not a villain. Ratna Singh was a noble person and knew how to treat senior but hapless ladies of the royal household. But for Meera, the really troublesome period started after Rana Ratna Singh's death in Samvat 1588 (1532 A.D.). At that time Meera was about 28. After Ratna Singh's death, the most vile and incompetent son of the great Rana Sangha, Vikramaditya, ascended to the throne.

He was given to all kinds of sensuous vices; he loved bragging and remaining all the time surrounded by sycophants. Being a bully by nature, he relished troubling the distressed and helpless people. His lecherous instinct was tempted by Meera's beauty and charms and he started making overtures towards her. But Meera, now totally immersed in devotion to her Sanwalia, couldn't care two hoots since she was unaware of all the worldly happenings. By then she had acquired a distinct aura of being an other worldly person, ever busy in welcoming Sadhus, composing poems for her Beloved Giridhar and doling out alms to the needy and the poor. She had become quite famous—'infamous' to many persons of the royal household—as the saintly poetess of incomparable charms. With the result, Vikram's overtures couldn't attract even her attention. Her total indifference to the new Rana made the Rana sting to the quick. 'How could a mere widow neglect the Rana' was the thought hammered into Rana's brain by his greedy sycophants. They egged on the Rana to teach this widow a lesson which she might remember for long. Although there were also faithful stalwarts of the old Rana's retinue who tried to dissuade the new Rana from stooping so low as to overpower a helpless widow, Vikram was in no mood to listen to their sane advice. Vikram was now growing increasingly arrogant due to his bad company. Ultimately he called his favourite sycophant and adviser, a money-lender of the Beeja-Vargi caste and together they hatched a vile conspiracy with the association of a lowly priest called Dayaram Panda. According to that vile trader of Beeja Vargi caste, the decision was taken to poison Meera so that the trouble could be rooted out finally.

While Meera was sitting before her Sanwalia, lost in her thought, all of a sudden a knock was heard at her door. Out emerged one of her maids to find Dayaram Panda who had considerably risen in the hierarchy of the royal household due to his closeness to the Rana.

"What has brought you here, O Brahmana Devata?" asked the maid quite respectfully.

"Is the queen present inside?" As the priest asked the question the maid also spotted a golden bowl covered with a platter in his one hand.

"Yes her highness is very much here. Why do you want her?" the maid, a confidant of the Queen Meera, asked rather suspiciously.

Before the priest could tell the reason he wanted to meet Queen Meera for, Meera herself reached near the gate. She heard the priest say: "His Highness, the Rana has sent this Charnamrita[1] of the Holy Lord Giridhara for the queen's consumption."

"What? The Rana has sent this divine potion for me!" Meera was quite thrilled. Of course she had been hearing about the various wicked tendencies displayed by the Rana, but she thought: 'A devotion to the Holy Lord can cleanse the mind of the most wicked persons and fill it with noble feelings.' With this thought uppermost in her mind she came ahead to accept the divine potion. And before the maid could do anything Meera took that bowl from Dayaram and went inside. She placed the bowl before her Lord 'Sanwalia' and concentrated her mind on the chosen lord. In no time the maid and Dayaram-who had also followed the queen inside the chamber, saw Meera's face radiating with a divine glow. And keeping her eyes closed and the mind concentrated on her Lord, Meera drank the potion with apparent delight.

---

1. This holy drink is made by washing the feet of the Chosen deity" (idol) with five sacred fluids including the curds, honey and milk etc.

As she imbibed it, the priest's whole body shuddered in an uncontrollable fright. The fire of remorse then began to singe his soul. While after drinking the potion, Meera was sitting quietly, the priest fell flat at her feet, crying:

"O Great Queen! This wasn't the divine portion but extremely toxic poison. It was the most deadly poison. O Mother! I was helpless to give it to you. The Rana made me bring this to you at the advice of the Beeja-vargi[1] money-lender." He kept on crying. But Meera was quite calm and composed. Her maid was too stupefied to express even shock at this outrage. Dayaram was weeping uncontrollably. Suddenly a song burst out of Meera's lips:

"Rana ji, the jahar diyo hai mhey jānee!
Jaise kanchana dehati agina main, nikasat barbanee!
Lok-laaj kula-kani jagat kee, dai bahaya jasa pānee!
Apne ghara ka parada kar ley, main abala baurānee!
Tarkasa teera lagyo mere hiyara, garake gayo sanakānee!
Sab santan par tana-mana baron, charan-kamal lapetānee!
Meera ko prabhu rakhi layee hai, dasee apanee jānee!"

[O Rana ji! I have detected that you had sent poison to kill me. But by facing this severe fire-test, only the purity of my love has been further vindicated. As gold when

---

1. According to a local legend of Rajasthan, Meera had detected that the potion contained deadly poison, sent by the Rana on that advice of the money-lender. Although the portion couldn't damage Meera, she cursed the whole clan of Beeja-vargi traders that their clan would perish. Still that clan of the traders of Rajasthan suffers that guilt which is believed to be the main reason of their never-ending adversities.

heated becomes purer, shedding out all its impurities and starts glittering with more radiating a glow, the same way my love passing through this test has become even firmer and much more pious. I seem to have shed all my misconceptions about the family prestige and honour as gold shed out its impurities on further heating. O Rana! (instead of caring for my fetterless behaviour), you should better care for the honour of your harem and make your queens stay behind the veils. Your these high-handed tactics would just cast no impression on me. I am just a hapless woman mad in love for my Lord. I have now dedicated everything I had in honouring the saints and holy men. But why should I care! I have been accepted by My Lord as his maid who has lovingly allowed me to stay wrapped around his lotus feet].

Concluding the song Meera rose up and moved steadily towards her bed. Dayaram was amazed. "Such a toxic poison and not even her walk is unsteady," he thought in utter disbelief and fell flat at Meera's feet seeking pardon. But Meera was hardly concerned. She beckoned her maid to take that fellow out and shut the door since now she was again in communion with her Sanwalia.

A bewildered Dayaram left, still wondering as to how could that deadly poison become the really divine potion for Meera. Her Sanwalia seemed to have converted deadly poison into an invigorating nectar! For Dayaram had himself detected that following her consumption of the 'Charnamrita' her face radiated with greater glow.

Was it really a miracle wrought by Meera's unflinching faith in her Sanwalia? Can deep devotion transform poison into nectar? Even now people ask these questions in disbelief, little realising that in the realm of true faith many such miracles are seen even in this age dominated by computer engendered scientific logic. Faith still dissolves even cancerous cells and cures the faithful. Some people who try to resolve this riddle through the means of scientific logic claim that gold vessels have the innate quality of neutralising the toxicity of the material contained by them. Quoting examples they assert that this was the reason, precisely, behind the grand Mughals and other emperors having their food and victuals supplied in gold vessels. It was not because of their desire to display their affluence so flamboyantly that they had their food in gold vessels; it was chiefly to ensure their eating unpoisoned food and drink. According to yet another apocryphal legend, a well-wisher of Meera had clandestinely altered the potion in the gold bowl before it was taken by Dayaram to Meera. Whatever the real reason be, the fact can't be denied even historically that Rana Vikram had sent poison for Meera which couldn't kill her.

Meera, on the other hand, was greatly delighted detecting her Sanwalia's hand in saving her life. That was the clear proof of her prayers reaching her chosen Lord. Enthralled by the unique experience Meera tied the tinkling anklet around her feet and started dancing in uncontrollable ecstasy:

Paga ghuhgharoo bandh Meera naachee re!
Main to apne Narayana kee, ape hee ho gayee dasee re!
Loga kahen Meera bhayee re bawaree, sasu kahe kula nasee re!
Visha ka pyala Rana ji bheja, peevat Meera hansee re!
Meera ke prabhu Giridhara Nagar, sahaj mile Avinasee re!

[This pada has been explained in detail ahead in the translated section. Suffice it to say here that this verse was apparently composed by Meera after this attempt to poison her by the Rana].

When the Rana heard about the failure of his attempt to eliminate Meera for good, he was stung to the quick. It was a searing blow to his swollen ego. 'A mere hapless widow could survive his carefully planned attempt to murder her? But how? Surely some of his confidants must have played the double game.' This thought made him all the more nervous and jittery. In a corner of his heart a thought did arise that Meera might really be a god-realised woman and hence he should go and seek pardon from hcr for his all vile attempts. 'But that would be accepting his unimitigated defeat before a mere widow', warned his ego. 'May be there was no divine intervention to upset his plans, but the outcome was due to the handiwork of some traitors', his ego persisted. So, despite an inner voice warning him to mend his ways, the mere thought of accepting his defeat before a woman, that too a widow, made his mind steeped in the traditional value that women are inferior, stick to the ego- gratifying path. With the resolve of taking the traitors to task after identifying them, he decided to make another careful attempt to slay Meera after some time. Meanwhile, he had to settle score with his traitors.

4

Meera Survives Further Attempts on Her Life

For Meera the life was as it had always been: full of innuendoes, aspersions, intrigues and conspiracies, but, undaunted by all these troubles, she continued to remain immersed in the love of her Sanwalia. Now she felt 'His' increasing presence all around her. She would hear the flute notes and now the rattling sound of someone dancing with the belled anklet's on one's feet. She would run helter-spelter only to find someone escaping her vision! Nevertheless, she was convinced that her Beloved Sanwalia was close by.

Meanwhile, Vikramaditya, the Rana, was still involved in hatching a plot to get rid of her. This time he devised a plan which might cause Meera's instant death. One of his advisers advised him to hide a cobra in a wicker-basket and send it to Meera through her close confidante, a maid. The maid was bought for very many temptations: gold, higher position and even land. That maid was, though initially a favourite of Meera yet she had fallen from grace when she was found to be indulging in amorous dalliance with a Rana's sepoy. Some scholars claim that that was also a part of the Rana's plot.

When Meera had just concluded her morning worship and was relaxing on the couch with her maid setting her hair, somebody knocked at the door of her private chamber. When the personal maid of Meera opened the gate at her mistress's bidding, she found the old maid of Meera standing there with a bundle covered in velvet. The person told Meera that the Rana had sent some special gift for her. Undaunted by the apprehensions Meera asked: "What's that?"

"I don't know, Rani ji!" the personal maid replied. "There is something kept in a covered wicker basket."

By this time the carrier of the basket had also come close. She said: "The Rana ji had received a precious Shaligram[1] stone. He thought that the best place to preserve it was near your Thakur ji!" Meera was delighted: "A Shaligram! Really? I am blessed! My Sanwalia keeps on giving me surprise gifts through various quarters." Thrilled with ecstasy on receiving something price-less, Meera eagerly removed the lid of the basket. While she had not yet completed the action, unable to control her emotions, the old maid who carried the gift, cried out: "Don't open, O Raani ji! Please! You may punish me with whatever punishment you deem fit. But the fact is that this basket does not contain a Shaligram but a deadly cobra," the maid couldn't hide her guilt.

---

1. A sacred stone worshipped by the Vaishnavas and supposed to be prevaded by the presence of Lord Krishna (or Vishnu), though biologically it is a black stone containing fossil ammonite.

But Meera lost in her thought, as though heard nothing. Despite the warning and request, she opened the basket without any fear. And so and behold! The basket indeed contained a priceless shining Shaligram stone. The maid who brought it, stood petrified there seeing the cobra turning into the holy stone. She fell flat at Meera's feet in utter supplication. Meera rose her up lovingly from the ground and pressed her close to her heart. Meera thanked the Rana profusely. Then the maid disclosed the entire plot[1]. Meera pardoned that old maid who then repaired straight to Vrindavan with a change of her heart.

All these events in Meera's life eminently reveal that she was subjected to all sorts of troubles by her in-laws yet she fearlessly continued to love her Lord. There were several events of such genre which occur in various folk-

---

1. This event is repeatedly referred to in Meera's 'Padas' for example, see the following couplets.

(a) Saanp pitaro Rana ji bhejyo, Meera haath diya jaya!
Hansa Hansa Meera kantha lagayo, yo mhare nausar haar!
[The Rana sent a poisonous snake to Meera which she lovingly and happily put it on her throat as though it was a precious pendant to her nine-layered costly necklace]

(b) Dabba kholle Meera jab dekhyo, ho gaye Saligram!
Jaya-jaya dhwani sab santa-sabha bhayee, kripa karee Ghanshyam!
[But when Meera opened the lid of the case she found a Shaligram there. The whole assembly of noble persons resounded the firmanent with the cries:" Victory! Victory! To Lord Ghanshyam! for showering such a grace upon her!]

(c) Mere Rana ji, main Govinda guna gaana!
Dabia men kali naag bheja, main Shaligram kar jana!
Meera prabhu ki prem-diwanee, main Sanwalia kar pana!
[O My Rana ji, I sing the noble virtues of Govinda (Krishna). You sent in a small case a dark snake but I found a Shaligram stone instead. Meera in the love of her 'Sanwalia' saw it as an hallowed emblem of her Lord.

lores of Rajasthan. There is enough material culled right from her poems to prove that her displaying her love to Sanwalia and leading an open, care free life, but her singing and dancing in the group of strange sadhus and holy men were not liked by the royal house-hold of Chittorgarh, particularly under the rule of Vikramaditya. But more the Rana tried to damage her or force her to behave in a proper manner, the more Meera grew determined to behave as she was behaving. Taunting upon the Rana's suspicious nature she has written:

Rana ji mhane ya badanami lage meethi!
Koyee nindo, koyee bindo, main chaloongee chal anoothee!

[O Rana! The infamy of mine which you spread is found to be sweet and likeable to me. Notwithstanding whether any one praises me or condemns me I shall continue to move on an incomparable path].

Apart from the Rana her sisters and mother-in-law also used to trouble her. It was a natural reaction to what she has had been supposedly doing. No house, let alone the royal house of the renowned citadel, Chittorgarh, could have tolerated such behaviour of a widow of the dead prince. Of course, Meera's female relations by marriage didn't go to the extent to which Rana had trangressed in his attempt to make Meera mend her ways', nevertheless, they did object to Meera's remaining veil-less and meeting the strange-saints and sadhus. Meera had repeatedly referred about the displeasure expressed by her sisters and mother-in-law. In one of her 'Padas' she has made a clear reference to the hardship suffered by her owing to the rigid norms of propriety maintained by the royal household. She writes:

Heli! Mhasoon Hari bin rahya na jaya!
Sasu lerhe meri nanada khijave, Rana rehyo risaya!
Paharo bhee rakhyo chaukee bithayo, talo diyo judaya!

[O Mate! I can't live without (remembering) Hari (Krishna) even though my mother-in-law picks on a fight with me on account of my this association and my sister-in-law reacts in a peevish manner while dealing with me, I can't mend my ways no matter how sorely the Rana sulks. They even put guards on me and had the sentinels placed before my gates to hold me captive with the locks shut on them, but I couldn't care less].

So determined was this lady that inspite of all fetters and restrictions she continued to move about in the company of strange sadhus and saints and love for her Sanwalia openly and unobtrusively in direct defiance of royal etiquette. At last, when her in-laws behaviour transcended all limits of decency, not out for fear for them but for securing peace of her own mind, she left Chittorgarh for good to visit places associated with Lord Krishna's sportive plays, including Vrindavan and Dwarka. Now she also longed to feel the ambience which her Lord might have experienced during his sojourns on earth as a human being.

hardship suffered by [illegible] on [illegible] to the [illegible] of [illegible] by the [illegible]

Hell, Mirza [illegible]

[illegible]

[illegible]

(10) [illegible] I can't live without [illegible] [illegible] [illegible] [illegible] [illegible] [illegible] [illegible] [illegible] them, but I couldn't comfort.

I determined [illegible] and [illegible] in the [illegible] [illegible] [illegible] [illegible] [illegible] [illegible] [illegible] [illegible] [illegible] [illegible] [illegible] [illegible]

5

Visit to Vrindavan and Dwarika and Her Coalescence With Her Lord

The problems faced by a beautiful widow determined to lead life in a gay-cavillier way could be well imagined in a traditional Hindu royal household about six hundred years back. Even now such permissions couldn't be granted, let alone then. With the result, having faced many attempts at her life together with other searing innuendoes and aspersions, Meera decided to leave Chittorgarh for good. She had no charm for the riches and authority and was not enamoured of being called a 'Rani'. Her only affluence was her love for the Sanwalia (Krishna). So she decided to visit Vrindavan, the eternal sportive ground for her Lord.

The Rana was no less pleased with Meera's this decision. 'Now she is herself planning to do what I should have done: kick out of Chittorgarh, this nautch girl!' so thought the Rana. With this thought in her mind he put no hurdles in the path of Meera's exit from Chittorgarh. Moreover, there were no propriety-hassels either since neither Meera had any son nor her husband had any issues from his previous wife. So there was no familial bond to force Meera stick to Chittorgarh.

Meera's decision to leave Chittorgarh for Vrindavan had many reasons behind it. Meera was getting sick of the opposition she had been facing in Chittorgarh. When she expressed a desire to do so, her holy companions asked her to go straight to Vrindavan. Right since the olden times, Vrindavan had come to be a shelter for the shelterless women. The tradition started way back at the fag end of the Dwapar Age and the beginning of the Kali Age, when Krishna decided to quit his mortal coil. For ensuring the safety and security of his women-folk, he had sent his chariot-driver, Daruk, to Arjuna in Hastinapur from Dwarka with the instructions to take the ladies of the Yadava household away from Dwarka and keep them in a secure place. But Arjuna could take them only half way when the tribals (Bhils) attacked the procession and took many of them away to the great surprise and chagrin of Arjuna. This mighty Pandava warrior who had defeated many a stalwart in the great war of Mahabharata, couldn't defeat the delinquent Bhils! Then Arjuna realised that the source of his strength was Krishna whose presence had really made them an invincible warrior team. This whole irony has been nicely highlighted by another Medieval Poet, Abdur-Rahim Khankhana, when he said in his famous Doha:

Rahiman nar ko ka bado, samaya bado balwan!
Bheelan lootee gopika, vehi Arjun vehi ban!!

[Says Rahim that it is not a man who is great or small but it is Time which favours or disfavours him. It is

Time that is all powerful otherwise how could the Bhils loot the Gopikas (Women of the Yadava family) when Arjuna was protecting them with his same powerful weapons as he has won the great war of Mahabharata with.]

It is believed that since then Vrindavan or Mathura has emerged as the only shelter for the shelterless women. But could Meera be considered 'shelterless' when her Sanwalia was there to look after her? Since her Sanwalia's place of sportive acts in the childhood (that was the image that Meera worshipped) was only Vrindavan, with her entourage of the saadhus and maids, she left Chittorgarh to reach Vrindavan via Pushkar.

Meera found it to be the best place in the world. Extolling Vrindavan's virtues, in one of her verses she admits:

"Ali Mhāne lage Vrindavan neeko!"

[O Mate! I found this Vrindavan to be a very good place[1]]

She was thrilled to be in Vrindavan. This is the only place in the entire world which is ever instinct with the devotion of Lord Krishna and his eternal beloved, Radha. Daily she would go to various temples and do her worship. For hours in the evening she would stay on the banks of the river Yamuna, imagining the sportive dalliance of her beloved 'Sanwalia' with the Gopis. It was at this place that she also came in the contact of a great saint Raidas and others. Meera's devotion to Krishna acquired further intensity. For many years she stayed here. Then, it is said, one day she felt as if her Lord was beckoning her to go to Dwarka, the

1. The text and translation of the whole verse is given ahead in the translation section.

final place of her Lord's dwelling on the earth. She then left for Dwarka visiting many teerathas on her way. Now she moved as the flow of a fetterless river swelling with love for her beloved and itching to meet the ocean, its soul-mate!

Meera was quite advanced in age by that time. But her love for her Sanwalia was still young and throbbing. In Dwarka she settled with her entourage and the centre of her worship was a small temple dedicated to 'Ranachod Das'. It is a typical name which literally means the one who flees from a battlefield. So great has been Lord Krishna's impact upon the Indian masses that even his negative attributes get extolled. This temple is a living example of that extreme popularity of the Lord. Isn't it amazing that even a deserter from the battlefield is lauded in loving affection?

The idol of the Lord in this place became the centre of devotion for Meera. Now she was too old to come to the temple daily and so she started staying there permanently. Now she longed for her eventual coalescence with her Lord. So one fine morning she, despite old age and feeble body, after offering her oblations to the Lord, started madly dancing before her "Sanwalia'. It is claimed that before many onlookers her entire body was, as if, absorbed by the image and she achieved her total coalescence with her Lord.

Although there is no authentic record of Meera's quitting her mortal coil, yet on the evidence of the available records and local legends her soul left for Vaikuntha between 1610 to 1613 Samvat (1556 to 1557 AD) at the age of around fifty.

6

The Places Associated With Meera

1. **Merata**: Also written as Merhata it is now a tiny town on the main line between Jaipur and Jodhpur. The station is called Merata Road. It is believed to be the native place of Meera. In the Medieval ages this was a stormy citadel of the Rathods, an off-shoot of the main dynasty that ruled from Jodhpur. Still the ruins of the Chaturbhuja temple built by Meera's ancestors Rao Doodaji exists. There is a small plaque among the ruins which claims it to be the birth place of Meera.

2. **Chittorgarh**: The most famous of all Rajpoot fortress towns, Chittorgarh has been a proud but silent witness to the bloodiest and rarest of the sacrifices in the form of Jauhars, the rituals of ceremonial self-immolation. Sacked thrice, Chittorgarh, the capital of Sisodias of Mewar, represents the quintessence of Rajpoot heroism and chivalry. This is a big fort covering an estimated 700 acres. One of the most lovingly preserved monument, in this fort is Meera temple. Near the Fateh Prakash Palace stands the Meera Temple. Meera Bai, as Meera is affectionately called in

Rajasthan and India, is said to have composed and sung her verses here in praise of Lord Krishna. The temple is encircled by an open colonnade with beautiful pavillions at the corner. That is the only monument of Meera in this ancient fort staying in which she had faced many an attempt on her life. On especial religious festivals like Holi or Janamashtami, bhajans by Meera are still sung here.

Chittorgarh is well connected by road with Jaipur (322 km), Ajmer (181 km) and Udaipur (112 km). A direct train links Chittorgarh to Delhi via Ajmer and Jaipur to Udaipur.

3. **Vrindavan**: 10 kms from Mathura, Vrindavan is too well known a holy place to require an introduction. It is so deeply associated with the cult of Krishna that the whole ambience appears ever instinct with the love for Radha and Krishna. But there is no monument indicating Meera's stay there. Easily approachable from Delhi by a variety of transport, it gathers devotees of Krishna from all over the world.

4. **Dwarka**: 'Dwarka' means the 'many gated' city. It is said to have been the capital of the Yadavas—whose leader was Lord Krishna —when they migrated to the western coast to avoid facing Jarasandha's attacks. It is believed that original Dwarka and four other succeeding it, are supposed to have been submerged into the Arabian Sea. The present Dwarka is the 6th city on the site. Dwarka is a sacred place and a centre of pilgrimage because of its association with Lord Krishna. The main temple here is Dwarikadhisha Temple which is a five storeyed edifice supported on 60 columns and is crowned by a soaring,

elaborately carved spire. Close to this temple is the temple dedicated to 'Ranachod Das' (Lord Krishna) which is believed to be the exact spot where Meera had coalesced herself with the idol, although barring the legend there is no monument signifying Meera's coming there and vanishing herself into the idol. Nevertheless, Meera's bhajans are regularly sung here.

7

Original Text, Romanised version And Hindi-English Simultaneous Translations of Meera's Famous Verses and Popular Songs

(i)
मीरां मगन भई हरि के गुण गाय

मीरां मगन भई हरि के गुण गाय ।
सांप पिटारा राणा भेज्या,
मीरां हाथ जब देखण लागी,
न्हाय धोय जब देखण लागी,
सालिगराम गइ पाय ।
जहर का प्याला राणा भेज्या,
अमृत दीन्ह बनाय ।
नहाय धोय जब पीवण लागी,
हो गइ अमर अंचाय ।
सूल सेज राणा ने भेजी,
दीज्यो मीरां सुलाय ।
सांझ भई मीरां सोवण लागी,
मानों फूल बिछाय ।
मीरां के प्रभु सदा सहाई,
राखे बिघन हटाय ।
भजन भाव में मस्त डोलती,
गिरधर पै बलि जाय ।

मीरां श्रीकृष्ण के गुणों का गायन करे आत्म-विभोर हो गई ।

राणा ने सांप को पिटारी में बन्द करके भेजा और कहा कि इसे मीरां के हाथ में दे देना । जब मैं नहा-धोकर उसे देखने लगी तो मैंने वहां सांप के स्थान पर शालिगराम की मूर्ति पाई ।

राणा ने मेरे प्राण लेने के लिए विष का प्याला भेजा परंतु प्रभु कृष्ण ने उसे अमृत बना दिया । जब मैंने स्नान-ध्यान करके उसे पिया तो मैं अमर हो गई ।

इसके पश्चात् राणा जी ने कांटो की सेज बनवा कर भेजी और कहलाया कि मीरां को इस पर सुला देना । संध्या समय जब मैं (मीरां) उस पर सोने लगी तो वह शूलों की सेज फूलों की मेज बन गई ।

(मीरां के) प्रभु गिरिधर नागर विघ्नों का निवारण करके सदैव मेरी सहायता करते हैं, इसलिए मैं भजन-भाव में मस्त होकर निर्भय विचरण करती हूँ तथा अपने गिरिधर गोपाल पर बार-बार न्यौछावर होती हूं ।

Meera Magan Bhayee Hari key Guna gaya

Meera Magan Bhayee Hari key Guna gaya

Saanp pitara Rana bhejya,
Meera haath diyo jaya;
Nhaya-Dhoya jab dekhan laagee
Sali gram gayee paya!
Jahar ka payala Rana bhejya,
Amrita deenha banaye;
Nhaya-Dhoya jab peevan laagee
Ho gayee amar anchaya
Soola sej rana ne bhejyo
Deejyo Meera Sulayo;
Samjhe bhayee Meera sovan lagee
Mano phool bichhaya!
Meera ke prabhu sada sahayee
Rakhey vighna hataya;
Bhajan Bhav men masta doltee
Giridhar pey bali jaya
Meera Magan Bhayee Hari key Guna gaya

Meera gets spell-bound while singing the glories of Lord Krishna. When Rana sent a deadly snake hidden in a closed bucket and I opened it after my bath and worship, I found the holy stone of Shaligram instead of the snake there. Then Rana sent a cup full of poison but my Lord converted it into nectar. When I drank it after my bath and worship, I became immortal imbibing it by the grace of the Lord. Subsequently, The Rana also sent a bed of thorns, with express instructions to make Meera lie on it. But in the (late) evening when she lied down on it, the thornful bed became a bed of flowers by His grace.

Since Meera's Lord, the lifter of the hill, the wise one, always removes obstacles and dangers from her way, she roams about fearlessly singing His praises and sacrificing every thing she has at the Lord's bidding.

(ii)
माई म्हां गोविंद गुण गाणा

माई म्हां गोविंद गुण गाणा ।

राजा रूठ्यां नगरी त्यागां,
हरि रूठ्यां कहं जाणा ।
राणौ भेज्या विषरी प्याला,
चरणामृत पी जाणा ।
काला नाग पिटारयां भेज्या,
सालगराम पिछाणा ।
मीरां तो अब प्रेम दिवाणी,
सांवलिया वर माणा ।

हे सखी! मैं तो गोविंद के ही गुण गाऊँगी ।

राजा के कुपित हो जाने पर तो मैं अपने नगर को छोड़कर आ गई हूँ । किंतु यदि मेरे स्वामी श्रीकृष्ण रूठ गए तो मैं कहां जाऊँगी । फिर तो मेरे लिए कोई स्थान ही शेष नहीं रहेगा।

राणा ने मेरे प्राण लेने के लिए मेरे पास विष से भरा हुआ प्याला भिजवाया था, जिसे मैंने श्री कृष्ण के चरणों का अमृत समझकर पी लिया ।

इसके बाद राणा ने पिटारी में बंद करके काला सांप भेजा । जब मैंने उसे खोला तो मुझे उसमें शालिग्राम प्राप्त हुए ।

मीरां तो अब श्रीकृष्ण के प्रेम में दिवानी हो गई है । मैंने सांवलिया कृष्ण को ही अपने प्रियतम के रूप में स्वीकार कर लिया है ।

Mayee! Mhan Govinda guna gana

Mayee! Mhan Govinda guna gana

Raja roothiyan nagri tayagan,
Hari roothiyan kahan jana!
Rana bhejya vish ro payala,
Charanamrita pee jana!
Kala nag pitaryan bhejya,
Shaligram pichana!
Meera to ab prem-diwanee,
Sanwariyan vara mana!
Mayee! Mhan Govinda guna gana

O Mate! Now I shall sing only Govinda's glories! When the king grew wroth I left the city and reached here. But should my master Lord Krishna be angry, where I would go? Then there would be no place where I can go?

When the Rana sent cup full of poison, I drank that gladly deeming it to have been water, my Lord's feet had been washed in.

Then the Rana also sent a black (deadly) serphant hidden in a closed basket but when I opened it I found a holy stone Shaligram* instead.

Meera is now madly in love with her chosen Lord Krishna whom she has finally accepted as her beloved.

---

* Shaligram : This stone is deemed by the devont Hindu to be permratus by Lord Vishnu (or Krishna's) presence. Actually it is a blackish stone containing fossil ammonite.

(iii)
मैने राम रतन धन पायो

मैंने राम रतन धन पायो ।

वस्तु अमोलक दी मेरे सतगुरु
करि किरिपा अपनायो ।
मैंने राम रतन धन पायो ।

जनम-जनम की पूंजी पायो,
जग में सबै खोबायो ।
खरचे नहिं, कोई चोर न लेवै,
दिन-दिन बढत सवायो ।
मैंने राम रतन धन पायो ।

सत की नाव खंवटिया सतगुरु
भव-सागर तरि आयो ।
मीरां के प्रभु गिरधर नागर
हरखि-हरखि जस गायो ।

मीरां कहती हैं कि मैंने राम नाम का परम धन प्राप्त कर लिया है। परम सम्पदा प्राप्त कर ली है ।

मेरे सतगुरु ने मुझे राम नाम की अमूल्य सम्पदा प्रदान की । (मुझमें तो कोई पात्रता भी नहीं थी किंतु सतगुरु ने) मुझ पर कृपा करके उन्होंने मुझे अपना बना लिया ।

मैंने जन्म-जन्मांतरों से अप्राप्य पूंजी को प्राप्त कर लिया और सांसारिक वासनाओं को पूरी तरह विस्मृत कर दिया । राम नाम की पूंजी ऐसी अद्भुत पूंजी है जो खर्च करने पर खर्च नहीं होती, इसे चाहकर भी कोई चोर चुरा नहीं सकता अपितु यह दिन-प्रतिदिन बढ़ती ही जाती है, सवाई होती जाती है ।

मीरां कहती हैं कि मैंने सत की नाव बनाई, सतगुरु उसका खेवटिया (माझी) था । उसने मुझे भवसागर से पार उतार दिया हे गिरिधर नागर कृष्ण ! तूने मुझे इतना दिया है कि अब तो मैं निरंतर प्रसन्नतापूर्वक तेरे यश का ही गायन कर रही हूं ।

Maine Ram Ratan Dhan Payo !

Maine Ram Ratan Dhan Payo !

Vastu amolaka di mere Satguru
Kari Kirpa apnayo!
Maine Ram Ratan Dhan Payo!

Janam-Janam Kee poonjee payo
Jag main sabei khobaayo!
Kharache nahin, koi chor na levey
Din-din badhat savaayo!
Maine Ram Ratan Dhan Payo!

Sata kee naava khewatiya Satguru
Bhav-sagar tari aayo!
Meera key Prabhu Giridhara Nagar
harakhi- harakhi jasa gayo!

Says Meera, I have recieved the ultimate wealth, the gem in the form of chanting Rama's name. It was my noble guru who helped me recieve this proce-less treasure [i.e.. he guided me to the Lord] and possess it as my very own.

I have, indeed, hit upon something achievable after many lives' difficult penance, a very rare achievement for anyone and, in the process, have uprooted and cast aside all the plants or shrurbs that had taken root in my heart. Now I have that gem whose yeild can never be exhausted no matter how liberally spent..It can neither be stolen. [On the contrary], it makes me grow richer and richer every day as it value enhances progressively.

Meera says that I had sailed across this sea of existence, making the essence of myself, the boat and my guru, the rower.. O Krishna, the lifter of the hill, You have given me so much that I now delightedly sing your glories without any concern whatever, non-stop.

(iv)
मै तो सांवरे के रंग रांची

मैं तो सांवरे के रंग रांची ।

साजि सिंगार, बांध पग घुंघरू
लोकलाज तजि नांची ।
गई कुमति, लई साधु की संगत
भगत रूप भई सांची ।

गाइ-गाइ हरि के गुन निसिदिन
काल-ब्याल सों बाची ।
उन बिन सब जग खारो लागत
और बात सब कांची ।

मीरां श्री गिरिधरन लाल सूं
भगति रसीली जांची ।
मैं तो सांवरे के रंग रांची ।

हे सखी! मैं तो सांवरे श्री कृष्ण के रंग में रग गई हूं । (अर्थात् उनके प्रेम में लीन हो गई हूं) ।

मैं सोलह शृंगार सजाकर, पैरों में घुघरू बांधकर, लोक-लज्जा को त्याग कर (प्रेम में उन्मुक्त होकर) नाची हूं । संत-संगति के प्रभाव से मेरा अविवेक समाप्त हो गया है, जिससे मैं सच्चे भक्त-स्वरूप को प्राप्त हुई हूं ।

रात-दिन श्रीकृष्ण के गुणों का गान करके मैं काल-रूपी सर्प से बच गई हूं (अर्थात् मोक्ष की अधिकारिणी हो गई हूं ।) अब तो श्रीकृष्ण के प्रेम का रंग मुझ पर ऐसा चढ़ गया है कि उनके बिना सारा संसार खारा (कटु) लगता है (अर्थात् निस्सार प्रतीत होता है ।) संसार के सारे प्रपंच क्षणभंगुर प्रतीत होते हैं ।

मीरां ने तो श्री गिरिधर गोपाल की आनंददायिनी प्रेमा-भक्ति की याचना की है । मीरां कहती हैं कि मैं श्रीकृष्ण के रंग में रंग गई हूं ।

Main to Sanware key Rang Raanchee

Main to Sanware key Rang Raanchee

Saaji shingara, bandha paga ghungharoo
Lok-laja taji naachee!
Gayee kumati, layee saadhu kee sangat,
Bhagata roop bhayee saanchee!

Gayee-gayee Hari key guna nisadina,
Kaal-byal son banchee!
Una bin sab jaga kharo lagat
Aur baat sab kaanchee!
Meera shree giridharan lal soon
Bhagat raseelee jaanchee!
Main to Sanware key Rang Raanchee

O Mate! I'm fully imbued in the shades of the Dark Complexioned [Krishna] [i.e.. I'm fully lost in his love.] Having decorated myself in all the sixteen modes, tying rattling anklets [ghungharoo] and throwing family pride and traditionas to winds I have freely danced, mad in love. Owing to my association with sages and sadhus my indiscreation has fled, leaving me as the true-devotee of my Lord.

I have been spread by the travails of the serpent Time since I passed my days and night only in the worship of my Lord [this way I deserve salvation as my soul is unaffected by mortal temptations]. Now my Lord's influence is so high over me that without him I can't stand this bitter world even in the imagination [i.e. the world is immaterial for me without him] which is very transistory and fey.

Meera has only demanded bliss-giving devotion to Lord, Gopal who lifted the mount and hence she is totally imbued in his complexion, (or possessed by His influnce.)

(v)
मै तो गिरधर के घर जाऊँ

मैं तो गिरधर के घर जाऊँ ।
गिरधर म्हारो साँचो प्रीतम
देखत रूप लुभाऊँ
रैन पड़े तब ही उठि जाऊँ ।
भोर भये उठि आऊँ
रैन दिना बाके संग खेलूं
ज्यूं-त्यूं ताहि रिझाऊँ ।

जो पहिरावै सोई पहिरूं
जो दे सोई खाऊँ ।
मेरी उनकी प्रीती पुरानी
उन बिन पल न रहाऊँ ।
जहां बैठावे तितहीं बैठूं
बेचै तो बिक जाऊँ ।
मीरा के प्रभु गिरधर नागर
बार-बार बलि जाऊँ ।

मैं तो अपने गिरधर गोपाल के घर जाऊँगी ।

गिरिधर कृष्ण ही मेरे सच्चे प्रियतम हैं । उनके रूप को देखकर मैं उनके प्रति मोहित हो गई हूं ।

अपने प्रियतम से मिलने के लिए मैं नित्य रात होते ही उनके पास चली जाउँगी तथा प्रातः होते ही लौट आऊँगी । मैं रात-दिन उनके साथ क्रीड़ा करूंगी और हर सम्भव उपाय से उन्हें रिझाऊँगी ।

वे मुझे जैसे भी रखेंगे, वैसे ही रह लूंगी । जो पहनाएंगे, पहन लूंगी । जो भी खिलाएंगे, खा लूंगी । मेरा और उनका प्रेम तो जन्म-जन्मांतरों का है । उनके बिना मैं एक पल के लिए भी नहीं रह सकती । वे मुझे जहां बैठाएंगे वहीं बैठ जाऊँगी । यदि वे मुझे बेचना चाहेंगे तो बिक भी जाऊँगी, (अर्थात मीरां अपने प्रियतम कृष्ण के प्रति पूरी तरह समर्पित है ।)

मीरां कहती हैं कि मेरे आराध्य तो वे गिरिधर श्रीकृष्ण हैं । उन पर मैं बार-बार बलिहारी हूं ।

Main to giridhara key ghara jaoon

Main to giridhara key ghara jaoon
Giridhara maharo sancho Preetam
Dekhata roop lubhaoon.
Reni pade tab he uthi jaoon
Bhor bhaye uthi aaoon
Ren-dina baake sang kheloon
Jyon-tyon tahi rijhaoon

Jo pahirave soyee pahiroon
Jo dey soyee khaoon
Meri unkee preeti puranee
Una bin pala na rahaoon
Jahan baithaye titaheen baithaoon
Bechei to bika jaoon
Meera key prabhu giridhar nager
Bar-bar bali jaoon!

I shall go to my Lord gopal's abode who mounted the hill [come what may.]

He is my true beloved. I have been captivated by His lovely form.

I shall go to Him as the night falls and return at the very dawn. This way I will enjoy my time with Him and employ every means to win Him over.

I will stay as He wants me to wear whatever He says and eat whatever he offers. My love with Him streches to many lives and hence I can't stay for even a second away from Him. I will sit wherever he asks me to and I would even accept my sale should he wish to do so. [i.e. I will be totally devoted to him word, deed and action].

Says Meera that "My Lord is Shree Krishna and I shall repeatedly sacrifice my life for his sake."

(vi)
मैं गिरधर के रंग राती

मैं तो गिरधर के रंग राती ।

पचरंग चोला पहर सखी मैं
झिरमिट खेलन जाती ।
ओह झिरमिट मां मिल्यो सांवरो,
खोल मिली तन गाती ।

जिनका पिया परदेस बसत है
लिख-लिख भेजे पाती ।
मेरा पिया मेरे हीय बसत है
ना कहूं आती जाती ।

चंदा जाएगा, सूरज जाएगा
जाएगी धरण अकासी ।
पवन पाणी दोनूं ही जाएंगे
अटल रहे अविनासी ।

हे सखी! मैं तो गिरिधर के प्रेम में रंग गई हूं ।

मैं पचरंगी चोला पहनकर झिरमिट खेलने जाती हूं । उसी झिरमिट के खेल में मुझे मेरा प्रियतम सांवरा श्रीकृष्ण मिलता है । जिसे देखते ही मैं अपना घूंघट हटाकर उससे आलिंगन-बद्ध हो गई ।

हे सखी! जिनके पति परदेश में रहते हैं, वे उन्हें पत्र लिख-लिखकर भेजती हैं । मेरा प्रिय तो मेरे हृद्‌य में निवास करता है इसलिए न मैं कहीं आती हूं और न कहीं जाती हूं । अर्थात् मैं जब चाहती हूं अपने हृद्‌य में विद्यमान प्रियतम के दर्शन लेती हूं ।

यह संसार क्षणभंगुर है । एक दिन ऐसा आएगा कि चांद, सूरज, धरती और आकाश सभी नष्ट हो जाएंगे । यहां तक पवन और पानी भी समाप्त हो जाएंगे । केवल अविनाशी ईश्वर ही विद्यमान रहेगा ।

Main Giridhara ke Ranga Ratee!

Main Giridhara ke Ranga Ratee!
Pacharanga chola pahara sakhee main
Jhirmita khelen jatee!
Oh, jhirmita maan milyo sanwaro
Khola milee tana gatee!

Jinka piya pardes basat hai
Likh-likh bhejye patee!
Mera piya mere heeya basat hai
Na kahoon aatee jatee!

Chanda jayega, sooraj jayega
Jayegee dharan akasee
Pavana paanee donoon hee jayenge
Atal rahe Avinasi!

My whole being now stands imbued in the shade of the Lord who mounted the hill. Donning this five shaded gown [i.e. the body with five senses I go to play 'Jhirmit' (i.e. come into the world) where during the play I happened to meet my beloved. The Dark Complexioned, Krishna. As I beheld Him I look away my veil and fell in a close embraces with him.

O Mate! They whose husbands stay abrcad maintain ther contact through writing letters to them. But my Lord and master stay within my heart. That is why I don't go out anywhere [and meet him when I want.]

This world is transistory and perishable. A day will dawn when all planets, sun, moon and even welkin will be destroyed. So much so that even water and air will also be absent. But then will still remain my Lord imperishable.

(vii)
मेरे तो गिरधर गोपाल

मेरे तो गिरधर गोपाल दूसरो न कोई ।
जाके सिर मोर-मुकुट मेरो पति सोई ।
छांड़ि दई कुल की कानि कहा करिहै कोई ।
संतन ढिंग बैठि-बैठि लोक-लाज खोई ।
अंसुवन जल सींचि-सींचि प्रेम-बेलि बोई ।
अब तो बेल फैल गई आनंद फल होई ।
दूध की मथनिया बड़े प्रेम से पिलाई ।
दधि मथि धृत काढ़ि लियो डारि दई छोई ।
भगत देखि राजी हुई जगत देखि रोई ।
दासि मीरा लाल गिरधर तारो अब मोही ।
मेरे तो गिरधर गोपाल दूसरो न कोई ।

गिरधर गोपाल कृष्ण के अतिरिक्त मेरा कोई नहीं है ।

जिनके सिर पर मोर-मुकुट सुशोभित है, वे ही मेरे पति हैं । उनके लिए मैंने कुल और वंश की मर्यादा भी त्याग दी है । अब मेरा कोई क्या करेगा?

संतों के निकट बैठ-बैठकर मैंने सामाजिक लज्जा को भी तिलांजलि दे दी है । मैंने अपनी प्रेम की बेल को अपने आंसुओं के जल से सींच-सींच कर पुष्ट किया है । अब तो प्रेम की यह बेल फैल गई है । पुष्पित और पल्लवित हो गई है । अब तो इस पर आनंद रूपी फल भी लगने लगा है ।

मैंने दूध जमाने के पात्र को बड़े प्रेम से बिलोया है । उसमें जमे दही को मथकर कृष्ण-प्रेम रूपी नवनीत को निकाल लिया है और छाछ रूपी निस्सार वस्तु को छोड़ दिया है । (अर्थात् संसार की निस्सार वस्तुओं के बीच मैंने कृष्ण-प्रेम रूपी सार तत्व को ही ग्रहण किया है ।)

कृष्ण के भक्तों को देखकर तो मुझे प्रसन्नता होती है परंतु संसार की रीति और परम्परा को देखकर अपार दुःख होता है । हे गिरिधारी! मीरां तो आपकी दासी है । इसे भवसागर से पार कीजिए ।

Mere to Giridhar Gopal

Mere to Giridhar Gopal Doosaro na koi!

Jake sir mor-mukut mero pati soyee!
Chhadi dayee kula kee kani kaha karihe koyee!
Santana dhing baithi-baithi loka-laja khoyee!
Asuvana jala seenchi-seenchi prem-Beli boyee!
Aba to beli phaili gayee ananda phala hoyee!
Doodh kee mathaniyan bade prem se biloyee!
Dadhi mathi ghrita kaadhi biyo, dari dayee chhoyee!
Bhagat dekhi rajee huye, jagat dekhi royee!
Daasi Meera lal giridhara, taro ab mohee!
Mere to giridhar gopal, doosra na koyee!

No one except the Gopal, who mounted the hill, is mine. He who has his head adorned with a crown wrought of peacock feathers is my husband. For him I have forsaken all the considerations concerning my family prestige and its honours. Now noone can damage me any further as I have nothing to lose.

Also sitting in the company of mendicants and sadhus I have also kicked off the norms of social etiquettes. The creeper of my love has been irrigated by the water of my eyes and now it has become strong and is spreading far and wide. [i.e. my love for Shri Krishna is now well known] Now it is bearing the flowers and fruits of pure bliss. I have stirred deeply the curds of love to extract butter [the devotion to Shri Krishna] from it. What now remains in it is the essence less material. [Meaning I have taken away the essence of the world, the devotion to Lord Shri Krishna, rejecting the waste material from the world.]

It is because of this essence with me that I rejoice seeing my fellow devotees and the devotees but sorrow at the seeing the people still adhering to meaningless hollow traditions and norms set by this fey world. O Lord who mounted the hill, now Meera is your maid! Please take her across the ocean of mortal world.

(viii)

मुरलिया बाजा जमना तीर

मुरलिया बाजा जमना तीर ।

मुरली म्हारो मन हर लीन्हीं,
चित्त धरां ना धीर ।

स्याम कन्हैया, स्याम कमरया,
स्याम जमन को नीर ।

धुन मुरली सुन सुध-बुध बिसरां,
जर-जर म्हारो सरीर ।

मीरां के प्रभु गिरधर नागर,
वेग हरयां म्हां पीर ।

जमुना के किनारे पर श्रीकष्ण की मुरली बज रही है ।

जब मुरली का मधुर स्वर गूंजता है तो वह मेरे मन को हर लेता है और तब मेरे हृद्य में धीरज शेष नहीं रहता ।

कन्हैया का नाम भी श्याम है, उनकी कांवरी भी सांवली जमुना का जल भी काला श्याम है ।

मुरली की ध्वनि सुन कर मैं अपनी सुध-बुध भूल जाती हूं और मेरा शरीर शिथिल हो जाता है ।

मीरां के स्वामी गिरिधर गोपाल! शीघ्र ही मीरां की पीड़ा दूर कीजिए ।

Muraliya Baja Jamuna Teer!

Muraliya Baja Jamuna Teer!

Muralee mharo mana hara leenho
Chitta dhare na dheer!

Shyam Kanaihiya, shyam kamarya
Shyam Jamuna ko neer!

Dhun muralee sun sudha-budha bisaree
jara-jara mharo sareer!

Meera ke prabhu giridhara nagar
Beg haryan mhan peer!

Muraliya Baja Jamuna Teer!

A flute is played on the bank of the river Jamuna [By the lord Krishna.]

Whenever the sweet notes resouned, they captivated my heart, making it lose its composure and go restless. Kanaihhya is dark, so is the garment on his body and so the waters of Jamuna.

Hearing the sweet notes emitted by the flute I lose my consciousness and my body also go uncontrollably lax.

O Meera's lord, Gopal, who lifted the hill, you must came before her quickly to relieve her of the agony she is suffering from.

(ix)
माई री मै तो लियो गोविन्दां मोल

माई री मैं तो लियो गोविन्दां मोल ।

कोई कहै छानै, कोई कहै चौड़े,
मैं तो लियो बजंता ढोल ।

कोई कहै महंगो, कोई कहै सुहंगो
मैं तो लियो तराजू तोल ।

कोई कहै कारो, कोई कहे गोरो
लियो री अमोलिक मोल ।

तन वारां मैं, जीवन वारां
वारां री अमोलक मोल ।

मीरां कूं प्रभु दरसन दीज्यो
पूरब जनम को कोल ।

सखी री, मैंने तो गोविन्द को मोल ले लिया है अथवा मैंने गोविन्द को सदा के लिए अपना बना लिया है ।

कोई कहता है कि मैंने यह प्रणय-व्यापार छिपकर किया कोई कहता है कि प्रकट में किया है । मैंने तो खुलेआम डंके की चोट पर प्रियतम श्याम का वरण किया है ।

कोई कहता है कि यह सौदा महंगा पड़ा है, कोई कहता है सस्ता मिला है । परन्तु मैंने तो तराजू से तोल कर (हानि-लाभ का पूरा विचार करके) श्याम-प्रेम का यह सौदा किया है ।

कोई कहता है कि मेरा प्रियतम सांवला है, कोई उसे गोरा कहता है, परंतु जो भी हो मैंने तो अमूल्य वस्तु मोल ले ली है ।

मैंने तो उन पर अपना तन और जीवन न्यौछावर कर दिया है और जीवन की अमूल्य वस्तु भी न्यौछावर कर दी है ।

मीरां के प्रभु! पूर्व जन्म में दिए गए वचन का स्मरण हुए अपनी इस प्रेम-दिवानी को दर्शन दीजिए ।

Mayee Ree ! Main to Liyo Govinda Mol

Mayee Ree ! Main to Liyo Govinda Mol
Koyee kahe chhane, Koyee kahe chaurhe;
Main to liye bajanta dhol!

Koyee kahe mehango, Koyee kahe suhango;
Main to liyo taraju tol!

Koyee kahe karo, Koyee kahe goro;
Liyo re amolaka mol!

Tana varan main, jeevan varaan;
Varaan ree amolaka mol!

Meera koon Prabhu darshan deejyo;
Poorab janam ko kol!

O mate! I have purchased Govinda (Shri Krishna) [against certain cost]. This way He shall ever be mine! Some say I indulged in this love trade clandestinely while others say it is an open deal. But I proclaim that; informing the whole world assertively, I have struck this deal and resoundingly made Govinda my own. [Yet people have their varied assessment of the deal.] Some say that it was an exorbitantly costly deal while others say it was cheap. But as far as I'm concerned I have weighed pros and cons carefully and only then have struck this deal with Shyam [Krishna].

Even the some say my beloved is too dark while some say that He is fair complexioned. But I, in the bargain, have recieved something truely price-less.

I have dedicated all that I possessed including my life to have him. I have given my all most valuable assets to have him as my husband. now, O Lord of Meera (since our union streches to many lives.)! recollecting your promise made in the previous lives to me, please appear before your devotee Meera, madly in your Love!

(x)
मने चाकर राखो जी

मने चाकर राखो जी ।
गिरधारी लाल चाकर राखो जी ।

चाकर रहसूं बाग लगासूं नित उठ दरसन पासूं ।
बृन्दावन की कुन्ज गलिन में तेरी लीला गासूं
मने चाकर राखो जी ।

चाकरी में दरसन पाऊँ सुमिरन पाऊँ खरची ।
भाव-भगति जागीरी पाऊँ तीनों बाता सरसी जी ।
मने चाकर राखो जी ।

मोर मुकुट पीताम्बर सोहै गल बैजन्ती माला ।
बृन्दावन में धेनु चरावे मोहन मुरली वाला ।
मने चाकर राखो जी ।

मीरां अपने आराध्य श्रीकृष्ण से निवेदन करती हुई कहती है कि आप मुझे अपनी सेविका बना लीजिए ।

सेविका बन कर मैं एक सुन्दर बाग बनाऊँगी और नित्य-प्रति उठने पर आपके दर्शन करूंगी । वृन्दावन की कुन्ज गलियों में घूम-घूम कर मैं आपकी लीला का गान करूंगी । आप मुझे अपनी सेविका बना लीजिए ।

आपकी सेविका बनने के बाद वेतन के रूप में मैं आपके दर्शन प्राप्त करूंगी । दैनिक व्यय के रूप में मुझे आपके स्मरण अवसर प्राप्त हो जाएगा । भाव और भक्ति की जागीर मुझे प्राप्त हो जाएगी । इस प्रकार मुझे दर्शन, स्मरण और भक्ति तीनों ही वस्तुएं प्राप्त हो जाएंगी । आप मुझे तो सेविका बना लीजिए ।

आपने अपने मस्तक पर मोर-मुकुट धारण किया हुआ है । आप के शरीर पर पीले वस्त्र सुशोभित हो रहे हैं । गले में वैजयन्ती माला शोभायमान है । मुरली बजाते हुए श्रीकृष्ण वृन्दावन में अपनी गायों को चरा रहे हैं ।

Mane Chakar Rakho Jee

Mane Chakar Rakho Jee
Giridhari Lal Chakar Rakho Jee!!

Chakar rahasoon bagh lagasoon Nita uthi Darshan pasoon;
Vrindavana kee kunj-galin mein Tere leela gasoon!
Mane Chakar Rakho Jee

Chakari main darshan paoon Sumiran paoon kharachee;
Bhav-bhagati jageeree paoon Teenon bata sarasee
Mane Chakar Rakho Jee

Mor-mukut peetambar sohe gala vaijayanti mala!
Vrindavana main dhenu charave Mohan muralee wala!
Mane Chakar Rakho Jee

Requesting her chosen deity Shree Krishna, Meera says that "O Lord! Make me your maid! Then I would lay a beautiful garden and every day would behold your visage. Moving about in the groves and lanes of Vrindavana I would sing your glories related to your sportive plays. Then in the form of daily wages due to your maid I would get your holy darshan and as allowance I would get the opportunity to concentrate my mind on to your visage. The estate of feeling and devotion would also be my lot. This way your darshan, rememberance and devotion shall be my great assets.

So, please appoint me as your maid. Then I behold your comely visage: with head adorned with peacock feathers crown. I would see you clad in yellow garments with the vaijayanti garland dangling around your neck and my Lord grazing the cows in Vrindavana forest, playing on his flute.

(xi)
भज मन चरण कंवल अविनासी

भज मन चरण कंवल अविनासी ।
जेताई दीसे धरण गगन बिच, तेताई सब उठ जासी ।
कहा भयो तीरथ व्रत कीन्हें, कहा लिए करवत कासी ।
या देही का गरब न करना, माटी में मिल जासी ।
यो संसार चहर की बाजी सांझ पड्या उठि जासी ।
कहा भयां है भगवा पहर्या, घर तज भए संन्यासी ।
जोगी होय जुगति नहिं जापी, उलटि जनम फिर आसी ।
अरज करो अबला कर जोरे, स्याम तुम्हारी दासी ।
मीरां के प्रभु गिरिधर नागर, काटो जम की फांसी ।

(अपने मन को संबोधित करती हुए मीरां कहती हैं कि) हे मन! तू अविनश्वर ईश्वर के चरण-कमलों की आराधना कर । धरती से लेकर आकाश तक जो कुछ भी दिखाई पड़ रहा है वह सब एक दिन नष्ट हो जाएगा ।

विभिन्न तीर्थो की यात्रा करने से, अनेक प्रकार के व्रत आदि करने से और काशी में जाकर आने से अपने शरीर को चिरवाने से भी कोई लाभ नहीं है । सुंदर शरीर को पाकर हमें गर्व नहीं करना चाहिए, क्योंकि यह शरीर भी एक दिन नष्ट होकर मिट्टी में मिल जाएगा ।

यह संसार चौपड़ की बाजी की तरह है । जिस प्रकार चौपड़ खेलने वाले शाम को अपनी बाजी बंद कर देते हैं उसी प्रकार इस संसार में आने वाले प्रत्येक व्यक्ति को कालरूपी संध्या के आने पर जाना पड़ता है ।

शरीर पर गेरुये वस्त्र धारण करने और घर को छोड़कर संन्यासी बन जाने से भी कोई लाभ होने वाला नहीं है । योग धारण करने पर भी यदि ईश्वर को प्राप्त करने की युक्ति नहीं पाती तो संन्यास लेना भी व्यर्थ हो जाएगा और पुनः इस संसार में जन्म लेना पड़ेगा ।

मीरांबाई अपने हाथ जोड़कर श्री कृष्ण से निवेदन करती हैं प्रभु मैं आपकी दासी हूं। आप मेरे स्वामी हैं । कृपया यम के फंदे को काटकर मुझे मोक्ष प्रदान कीजिए ।

Bhaja man charan kanwal Avinashi!

Bhaja man charan kanwal Avinashi!
jetayee deese dharan-gagan bich Tetayee sab utha jasee!

Kaha bhayo teerath vrata keenhan kaha liye karvat kaashi!
Ya dehi ka garab na karna Mati main mil jasee!

Yo sansaar chahar ki baaje Sanjha padya uthi jasee!

Kahan bhayan hai bhagwa paharya
ghara taja bhaye sanyasi!
jogi hoye juguti nahin japee Ulti janam phir assee!

Araja karo abla kar jore Syam tumhari dasee!
Meera ke prabhu Giridhara nagar
kato jama kee phansee!

[Addressing her mind Meera says] Mind! Worship only the lotus feet of the Imperishable Lord! For whatever you behold between earth and sky shall vanish one day.

No use visiting pilgrim centres, keeping difficult penances and fast and meeting one's death through the blade in Kaashi*. One shouldn't be proud of this fey body which has to vanish in the debris of dust.

This world is like game of dice closed every day at sun-set. the same way each one meets one's sun-set. No use either leaving home donning saffron mobes or mastering yoga since failure in any such attempt would make rebirth compulsory in this very world. Hand bound Meera prays: "O Lord! I'm thine maid and you the master! Please cut my mortal bonds and let my soul get salvation."

---

* A particular ritual, akin to commiting suicide, used to be held to ensure salvation to the dying man's soul.

(xii)
बादर देख डरी हो, स्याम

बादर देख डरी हो स्याम ।
मैं बादर देख डरी ।

काली-पीली घटा उमड़ी
बरस्यो एक घरी ।
जित जाऊँ तित पानि ही पानी
हुई सब भूमि हरी ।

जाका पिव परदेस बसत है,
भीजै बार खरी ।
मीरां कै प्रभु गिरधर नागर
कीज्यो प्रीति खरी ।

हे कृष्ण! आकाश में उमड़ते-घुमड़ते बादलों को देखकर मैं भयभीत हो गई हूं । ये काले-काले बादल मुझे बहुत डरा रहे है ।

काली-काली घटाएं चारों ओर उमड़ने लगती हैं और कुछ देर बरसने के बाद समाप्त हो जाती हैं । इसके बाद मैं जिधर भी जाती हूं, उधर पानी ही पानी दिखाई देता है । सारी धरती हरी भरी हो गई है ।

जिनके प्रियतम परदेश में रहते हैं, वे वियोगिनियां अपने प्रियतम की प्रतीक्षा में खड़ी-खड़ी भीग रही हैं । मीरां अपनी अनन्य भक्ति का परिचय देते हुए कहती हैं कि मेरे आराध्य गिरिधर गोपाल! आप मेरे प्रति अपनी प्रीति को खरी सिद्ध कीजिएगा अर्थात् इस पावस ऋतु में आकर अपने प्रेम की सच्चाई सिद्ध कीजिएगा ।

Badar dekh daree ho, Shyam!

Badar dekh daree ho, Shyam!
Main badar dekh daree!

Kaali-peeli ghata oomadee
Barsyo ek gharee
Jita jaoon tita pani hee pani
Huyee sab bhoomi haree!

Jaake piva paradesh basat hain
Bheejen bar kharee!
Meera ke prabhu Giridhara Nagar
Keejyo Preeti kharee!

Hey Krishna! I am frightened seeing the dark clouds gathering all around. These dark(rain-ladein) clouds are causing me a great fear.

These dark clouds gather and scatter after pouring down rain for sometime. Thereafter, wherever I behold I see water and water with whole ground becoming verdant and green.

Those love-lorn dames whose husband are abroad wait in the rain endlessly and get drenched. [Says Meera asserting the purity of her love.] O my Chosen Lord, Gopal, who mounted the hill, it is high time you too vindicated your love for me in this beautiful season.

(xiii)
बसो मोरे नैनन में नंदलाल

बसो मोरे नैनन में नंदलाल ।

मोहनि मूरत, सांवली सूरत
नैना बने बिसाल ।
अधर सुधारस मुरली राजति
उर बैजन्ती माल ।
बसो मोरे नैनन में नंदलाल ।

छुद्र घंटिका कटि तट सोभित
नूपुर सबद रसाल ।
मीरां-प्रभु संतन सुखदाई
भक्त बछल गोपाल ।
बसो मोरे नैनन में गोपाल ।

हे नंदनंदन कृष्ण! आप मेरे नयनों में निवास करो । (अर्थात् आपकी रूपमाधुरी मेरी आंखों में सदैव बसी रहे ।)

आपका रूप अत्यधिक मोहक है । आपकी सूरत सांवली-सलोनी है । आपके नेत्र बड़े-बड़े हैं ।

आपके ओठों पर अमृतरस बरसाने वाली मुरली सुशोभित है अथवा आपके सुधारस से परिपूर्ण अधरों पर मुरली शोभित है आपके वक्ष पर वैजयंती माला अत्यधिक रुचिकर लग रही है ।

श्री कृष्ण की कमर में छोटी-सी घंटी और पैरों में सरस व मधुर ध्वनि उत्पन्न करने वाले घुघंरू सुशोभित हैं । मीरां कहती हैं कि मेरे प्रभु संतों को सुख देने वाले हैं और भक्तों से प्रेम करने वाले हैं । ऐसी मनोहर छवि वाले श्रीकृष्ण मेरे नेत्रों में आकर बस जाएं ।

Baso More Nainana main Nandalal

Baso more nainana main Nandalal!

Mohini moorat, sanwali soorat
Naina bane bisaala!
Adhara sudharas Murali rajati
Ur vaijayanti mala!
Baso More Nainana main Nandalal!

Chhudra ghantika kati tata shobhit
Noopur sabad rasal!
Meera- Prabhu santan sukh-dayee
Bhakta-bachhala gopal!
Baso More Nainana main Nandalal!

O Krishna, son of Nanda! Kindly ever dwell in my eyes [i.e. your cameliness may ever remain available to my vision].

Your appearence is very captivating. Your dark and smooth complexioned body and your big eyes. Bedight upon your lips is that flute that rains nector through its melodious notes and on your bosom gleaming a most attractive vaijayanti garland.

In the waist are tied small bells and on feet the rattling anklets that produce very sweet sound. Says Meera bai that "My Lord is bestower of happiness to all those of noble nature and he loves his devotees immensely. Let Krishna with such captivating form may ever dwell in my eyes".

(xiv)
बरसे बदरिया सावन की

बरसे बदरिया सावन की ।
सावन की मनभावन की ।

सावन में उमग्यो मेरो मनवा,
भनक सुनी हरि आवन की ।

उमड़-घुमड़ चहुं दिसि से आया,
दामिनि दमके झर लावन की ।

नन्हीं-नन्हीं बूंदन मेहा बरसे,
शीतल पवन सोहावन की ।

मीरा के प्रभु गिरधर नागर,
आनन्द-मंगल गावन की ।

सावन की बदलियाँ बरस रही है । यह मनभावन सावन की बदरिया है ।

ऐसे सावन में प्रियतम कृष्ण के आगमन का समाचार कानों में पड़ते ही मेरा मन उमंग से भर उठा है ।

चारों ओर से बादल उमड़-घुमड़ कर छा गए हैं तथा वर्षा आगमन की सूचक बिजलियां चमक उठी हैं ।

बादलों से नन्हीं-नन्हीं बूंदों के रूप में वर्षा की फुहारें झरने लगी हैं तथा शीतल-सुहावन हवा चलने लगी है ।

मीरां के प्रभु गिरधर नागर! मेरे लिए तो यह आनन्द और मंगल के गीत गाने का क्षण है ।

Barse Badariya Sawan Ki

Barse Badariya Sawan Ki!
Sawan ki man-bhawan ki!

Sawan main Umgyo mero manava
Bhanak sunee Hari awan ki!

Umadh-ghumad chahun disi se aya
Damini damake jhara lawan ki

Nanhi-nanhin boondana meha barase
Sheetal pawan suhawan ki

Meera ke prabhu Giridhara Nagar
Anand-mangal gavan ki!

The clouds of sawan (the wettest month) are pouring down rain. These clouds are heart-bewitching.

During this pleasent season my heart grew ecstatic the moment I heard the good news of my beloved* (Krishna's) arrival.

The clouds have gathered thickly all over the sky and flash of lightning indicating the onset of heavy rain.

Tiny droplets from the clouds have already started falling down with cool and pleasent winds have also started to blow.

O Meera's beloved Lord, the wise one who lifted the mount, for her it is an hour to sing the odes of gratulation and rejoice greatly.

---

* Seeing the dark clouds Meera is reminded of her Beloved Krishna's dark complexioned body. Hence the ecstasy.

(xv)

बरजी मैं काहू की नाहिं रहूं

बरजी मैं काहू की नाहिं रहूं ।
सुनो री सखी तुमसों या मन की
सांची बात कहूं ।

साधु-संगति कर हरि सुख लेऊँ,
जगतें हौं दूरि रहूं ।
तन-मन-धन मेरो सब ही जावो,
भल मेरो सीस लहूं ।

मन मेरो लागो सुमिरन सेती,
सबका मैं बोल सहूं ।
मीरां के प्रभु गिरधर नागर,
सतगुरू शरण गहूं ।

मैं किसी के रोके न रुकूंगी । हे सखी, सुनो! मैं तुमसे अपने मन की सच्ची बात कहती हूं ।

मैं साधु-सन्तों की संगति में ही कृष्ण-भक्ति का सुख प्राप्त करती हूं तथा सांसारिक प्रपंचों से दूर रहती हूं । इसके लिए चाहे मेरा तन, मन, धन सब कुछ चला जाए, चाहे कोई मेरा मस्तक ही काट ले परन्तु मैं इससे विमुख नहीं हो सकूंगी ।

मेरा मन तो अब पूर्ण रूप से अपने आराध्य श्रीकृष्ण के ध्यान में लग गया है । इसके लिए मैं संसार-भर के सारे उपालंभ और ताने सह लूंगी । मीरां के स्वामी गिरिधर नागर, मैंने अब सत्गरु की शरण ग्रहण कर ली है ।

Baraji Main kahoo ki Nahin Rahoon

Baraji Main kahoo ki Nahin Rahoon!
Suno ree sakhi tumson ya mana kee
Saanchi Baat kahoon!

Saadhu sangati kara hari sukh leoon
Jagaten hon doori rahon
Tana-Mana-Dhana mero sab he javo
Bhala mero seesa lahoon!

Mana mero lago sumiran seti
Sabaka main bol sahoon!
Meera ke prabhu giridhara nagar
Sataguru sharan gahoon!

My Mate, listen! I tell you a honest resolve of my heart: no matter who prevents me from proceeding on my chosen path, I won't stop.

I derived happiness out of enjoying the devotion to my Lord Krishna even in the company of noble saints and holymen. This way I stay away from the various allurements of the world. No matter I lose everything my mind's peace my body's comfort or my entire wealth even my head but I shall never turn away from the path.

My mind is now totally devoted to thinking about my chosen Lord Krishna. For maintaining my this resolve I would gladly tolerate all the incentives and abuses hurled towards me. Now by the grace of Meera's Master, the exalted lord who mounted the hill, I have recieved shelter under my this noble guru.

(xvi)
प्रभु सों मिलन कसे होय

प्रभु सों मिलन कसे होय ।

पांच पहर धन्धे में बीते;
तीन पहर रहे सोय ।
मानुस जनम अमोलक पायो,
सोतें डार्‌यो खोय ।
मीरां के प्रभु गिरधर भजीये,
होनी होय सो होय ।

(मीरां अपने मन में चिन्तन करती हैं कि) प्रभु से किस प्रकार मिलन हो सकता है? पांच पहर तो काम-काज में बीत जाते हैं और तीन पहर सोकर समाप्त हो जाते हैं ।

हमने मानव का अमूल्य जन्म प्राप्त किया किन्तु इसे सोकर बेकार कर डाला ।

मीरां कहती हैं कि प्रभु गिरिधर नागर का ही भजन और उनका कीर्तन करना चाहिए । जो हमारे भाग्य में लिखा है, वह तो होकर ही रहेगा, इसलिए उसकी चिन्ता नहीं करनी चाहिए ।

Prabhu son Milan Kase Hoya

Prabhu son Milan Kase Hoya!

Pancha pehar dhande men beetey
teena pehar rahe soye!
Manas janam amolaka payo
Soten darayo khoye!
Meera ke prabhu giridhara nagar
Honee hoya so hoya!

[Reflecting in her mind Meera says] How can I meet the Lord? Three fourth of the day we pass in every day in business occupations and the rest in sleeping.

Though we are born in the precious and rare human species but we have destroyed the oppurtunity by sleeping and wasting it this way.

Says Meera that one should keep one's mind devoted in singing glories of wise Lord, who lifted the hill and thinking about him only. Since destiny is immutable we shouldn't worry about what is going to happen. [All that is destined is bound to happen, so why should we waste our time in thinking over it.]

(xvii)
प्रभु जी थे कहां गया

प्रभु जी! थे कहां गया
नेहड़ो लगाय ।

छोड़ गया विस्वास संगाती
प्रेम की बाती बराय ।

बिरह-समंद छोड़ गया छो
नेह की नाव चलाय ।

मीरां के प्रभु कबरे मिलोगे,
तुम बिन राह न जाय ।

हे स्वामी! तुम मुझ से प्रेम-सम्बन्ध स्थापित करके कहां चले गए हो?

हे विश्वासों के साथी! तुमने मेरे विश्वास को ही तोड़ दिया । मेरे हृद्य में प्रेम की लौ लगा कर मुझे छोड़ दिया । (मेरे प्राणों में प्रेम की वर्तिका जला कर तुम मुझ से विमुख हो गए ।)

(हे निष्ठुर क्या प्रेम की यही रीति है कि) प्रीति नाव चला कर तुमने मुझे विरह के सागर में बेसहारा छोड़ दिया है ।

मीरां कहती हैं कि हे प्रभु! तुम कब मिलोगे? तुम्हारे बिना रहना कठिन हो गया है।

Prabhu Jee! the kahan gaya

Prabhu Jee! the kahan gaya
Nehro Lagaaya!

Chhoda gaya biswas sangatee
Prem kee batee baraya!

Birah-samanda main chhod gaya chho
Neha kee nava chalaaya!

Meera ke Prabhu kabre miloge
Tum bin rahya na jaya!

O Master! Where have you vanished to after establishing relations of love with me?

O my close Confidant! You seem to have broken my confidence yourself. Having kindled the flame of love in my heart you have deserted me.!

O heartless! This is not the proper way of loving one. You seem to have left me supportless in the sea of seperation after having rowed my love-boat to a few paces.

Says Meera, O Lord! When will you meet me now? It is difficult for me to survive now in your absence!

(xviii)
पिय इतनी विनती सुनि मोरी

पिय इतनी विनती सुनि मोरी
कोई कहियो रे जाय ।

औरन सूं रस बतियां करत हो
हम से रहे चित चोरी ।
तुम बिन मेरे और न कोई
मैं सरणागत तोरी ।
पिय इतनी विनती सुनि मोरी ।

आवण कह गए अजहूं न आये
दिवस रहे अब थोरी ।
मीरां के प्रभु कब रे मिलोगे
अरज करूं कर जोरी ।
मिया इतनी विनती सुनि मोरी ।

कोई व्यक्ति मेरे प्रियतम से जाकर इतना भर कह दे कि मेरी विनती को सुन लें ।

(अपने प्रियतम को उलाहना देती हुई मीरा कहती हैं) तुम दूसरों के साथ हंस-हंसकर प्रेम की बातें करते हो किंतु हमसे ही अपना चित्त चुराये रहते हो । (अर्थात् तुम निरंतर हमारी उपेक्षा करते रहते हो ।) हे प्रभु! आपके अतिरिक्त मेरा और कोई सहारा नहीं है । मैं आपकी शरण में हूं ।

हे प्रभु! आप शीघ्र आने का वचन देकर गए थे, किंतु इतना समय बीत जाने पर भी लौटकर नहीं आए हो । अब तो मुझे अपने जीवन का भी कोई भरोसा नहीं रहा है। मेरे जीवन के अब थोड़े से दिन शेष रह गए हैं । प्रभु! मैं आपसे करबद्ध प्रार्थना कर रही हूं । मुझे आप शीघ्र बताएं कि आप अब अपने दर्शन कब देगे?

Piya Itni Binatee Suni Moree

Piya itni binatee suni moree!
Koyee kahiyo re jaaya!

Auran soon rasa batiyan karat ho
hum se rahe chita chori
tum bin mere aur na koyee
main sharanagat toree!
Piya Itni Binatee Suni Moree1

Aavana kahi gaye, ajahoon na aye
Diwas rahe ab thore
Meera ke prabhu kab re miloge
Araja karoon kara joree!
Piya itni binatee suni moree!

Let someone tell my beloved to listen to my supplication. You talk with others quite lovingly but always keep your mind withdrawn from me. [i.e. you ever neglect me.] O Lord! no one except you can provide me any support. So I seek your solitary shelter.

Lord! You had promised to return soon but haven't returned after such a long gap. Now I'm not even sure of living till your return since my days are numbered. Lord! Handbounded I request you to tell me as to when my eyes will behold you!

(xix)
पग घुंघरू बांध मीरा नाची रे

पग घुंघरू बांध मीरा नाची रे ।

मैं तो अपने नारायण की
आपहिं हो गई दासी रे ।
लोग कहें मीरां भई बावरी
सासु कहें कुल नासी रे ।
पग घुंघरू बांध मीरा नाची रे ।

विष का प्याला राणाजी भेज्या
पीवत मीरां हांसी रे ।
मीरा के प्रभु गिरधर नागर
सहज मिले अविनासी रे ।
पग घुंघरू बांध मीरा नाची रे ।

अपने सांवलिया श्री कृष्ण के प्रेम में तन्मय होकर मीरां अपने पैरों में घुंघरू बांध कर नाचने लगीं ।

मीरां कहती हैं कि मैं तो अपने आराध्य प्रभु श्रीकृष्ण की आप ही दासी हो गई हूं। (तात्पर्य यह है कि उनके प्रेम के वशीभूत होकर मीरां ने उन्हें सर्वस्व अर्पित कर दिया है ।) संसार कहता है कि मीरां पागल हो गई है । सासु कहती है कि मीरां कुल-मर्यादा को नष्ट कर रही है ।

राणाजी (मीरां के देवर विक्रमादित्य) ने मीरां के प्राण लेने के लिए उसके पास विष से परिपूर्ण प्याला भेजा किन्तु मीरां ने उसे हंसते-हंसते पी लिया । मीरां के प्रभु तो गिरिधर नागर श्रीकृष्ण हैं और वह अविनाशी कृष्ण उसे सहज ही सरलता से प्राप्त हो गए हैं ।

Paga Ghungharoo Bandha Meera Nachee Re

Paga ghungharoo bandha meera nachee re!

Main to apne narayan kee
apahin ho gayee dasee re!
Loga kahen Meera bhayee bawaree
Sasu kahen kula nasee re!
Paga ghungharoo bandha meera nachee re!

Visha ka pyaalaa Ranajee bhejya
Pewat Meera hansee re!
Meera ke prabhu Giridhara Nagar
Sahaj mile Avinashi re!
Paga ghungharoo bandha meera nachee re!

Lost in the love of her Dark Complexioned Beloved, Meera, tying bells endowed anklets, has started to dance.

Says Meera that I have become a slave of my beloved Lord Krishna as if without any effort. [i.e. The love of Lord has so possessed Meera that she has offered her entire self to the Lord's service.] Now, while the world alleges that Meera has grown mad, her mother-in-law complaints that Meera is ruining the family prestige.

The Rana (Meera's brother-in-law, Vikramaditya)sent a poison filled cup to meera to cause her death but she drank it happily, without a ditch and nothing happened to her. [It is because] Meera's Lord is Shree Krishna, the wise, who lifted the hill, and that Lord is now easily accessible to her.[Hence her this ecstasy!]

(xx)
दरस बिन दूखन लागै नैन

दरस बिन दूखन लागै नैन
जब से बिछु ड़े मोरे प्रभु जी,
कबहुं न पायो चैन ।

सबद सुनत मेरी छतियां कंपै,
मीठे लागै बैन ।
विरह-बिथा कासूं कहूं सजनी ।
बह गई करवत-अैन ।

कल न परत, हरि मग जोवत,
भई छमासी रैण ।
मीरां के प्रभु कबरे मिलोगे,
दुःख मेटण सुख दैण ।

हे प्रभु! आपके दर्शन के बिना मेरी आंखें दुखने लगी हैं । जब से आपका वियोग हुआ है, तब से मुझे एक पल का भी चैन नहीं मिला है ।

आपके मधुर वचनों का स्मरण आते ही मेरा हृद्य कांपने लगता है । आपके प्रेमपूर्ण शब्दों को सुन कर मैं पुलकित हो उठती हूं । मैं अपनी विरह-व्यथा किससे कहूं। मुझ पर तो जैसे करवत ही चल गई है कि मुझे विरह ने पूरी तरह से घायल कर दिया है ।

प्रभु के बिना मुझे एक पल भी चैन नहीं मिलता है । रात दिन मैं उन्हीं की बाट जोहती रहती हूं । उनके वियोग में रात भी छह मास जितनी लम्बी हो गई है । मीरां कहती हैं कि हे प्रभु! आप मुझ से कब मिलोगे । आप ही तो मेरे दुःखों को मिटाने वाले और सुखों को देने वाले हैं ।

Daras Bin Dookhana Lage Naina

Daras Bin Dookhana Lage Naina!
Jabase bichhure more Prabhu jee
Kabahoon na payo chaina!

Sabad sunat meri chhatiyan kamke
Meethe lage baina!
Birah bitha kasoon kahoon Sajani
Baha gayee karbat-eina!

Kala na parat, Hari maga jowat
Bhayee chhamasee raina!
Meera ke Prabhu kabare miloge
Dukh metana sukh daina!

O Lord! without beholding your comely form my eyes have begun to ache. Right since the time I have come in the separation from you I have failed to recieve a moment's relief.

Recollecting your sweet words my heart gets disturbed. Those love-filled words make a thrill pass through myself. But before whom should I relate the tale of my woe. I feel as though a fine-edged sword has wounded my heart. [i.e. I am, totally distressed with the agony of separation from my Lord.]

The absence of my Lord doesn't allow me even a moment's relief. Day in and day out I wait for his arrival; in separation from him a night has seemingly elongated as much as to cover six months time. Meera, 'O MyLord ! When would you meet me since you are the sole redeemer of my distress and bestower of happiness to me

(xxi)
थे बिण म्हांरे कोण खबर ले

थे बिण म्हारे कोण खबर ले,
गोवरधन गिरधारी?

मोर मुकट पीताम्बर शोभां,
कुण्डल री छब न्यारी ।

भरी सभां मा द्रुपद सुतारी,
राख्या लाज मुरारी ।

मीरां रे प्रभु गिरधर नागर,
चरण कंवल बलिहारी ।

गोवर्धन पर्वत को धारण करने वाले हे प्रभु! श्री कृष्ण के बिना मेरी खोज-खबर लेने वाला कोई भी नहीं है ।

आपके मस्तक पर मोर का मुकुट शोभायमान है । आपने पीले वस्त्र धारण किए हुए हैं । कानों में कुण्डल अत्यधिक सुन्दर लग रहे हैं ।

आपने ही भरी सभा में राजा द्रुपद की पुत्री द्रौपदी का चीर बढ़ा कर उसकी लज्जा की रक्षा की थी ।

मीरां के प्रभु! मैं आपके चरण-कमलों पर स्वयं को निछावर करती हूँ ।

Then Bin Mhare kon khabar le

Then Bin Mhare kon khabar le!
Goverdhna Giridharee?

Mor-mukut peetambar shobhan
Kundal ree chaba nyaree!

Bharee sabha maan Drupada suta ree
Rakhya laaj Murari!

Meera ke Prabhu Giridhara nagar
Charana kamal baliharee!

O Lord! who mounted the hill of Goverdhana! None except you is here to care for me. You have your head adorned with the crown wrought of the peacock's feathers. You are clad in yellow clothes and the ear-ring on your ears look very captivating.

It was you who in the open court filled to capacity that had saved the honour of the King Drupuda's daughter by enhancing the length of the cloth she was covered by!

O Lord of Meera ! I offer myself for the sacrifice at your lotus-like feet.

(xxii)
थे तो पलक उघाड़ो दीनानाथ

थे तो पलक उघाड़ो दीनानाथ,
मैं हाजिर-नाजिर कब की खड़ी ।

साजनियां दुसमन होय बैठ्या,
सबने लगूं कड़ी ।
तुम बिन साजन कोई नहीं है,
डिगी नाव समंद अड़ी ।

दिन नहिं चैन, रैन नहिं निदया,
सूखूं खड़ी-खड़ी ।
बाण विरह का लग्या हिये में,
भूलूं न एक घड़ी ।

पत्थर की तो अहिल्या तारी,
बन के बीच पड़ी ।
कहां बोझ मीरां में कहिए,
सौ पर एक धड़ी ।

हे दीनानाथ! अब तो आप मेरी ओर कृपा की दृष्टि डालिए । मैं आपकी सेवा में कब से उपस्थित हूं ।

सभी सगे-सम्बन्धी मेरे दुश्मन बने बैठे हैं । मैं सभी को बुरी लगती हूं । हे प्रिय! आपके अतिरिक्त मेरा कोई अपना नहीं है । आप ही मेरे प्रियतम हैं । मेरी जीवन-नौका डगमगाती हुई भव-सागर में अटक गई है । अब आप ही मुझे पार लगाइए ।

मुझे दिन में भी आराम नहीं मिलता और रात में भी नींद नहीं आती है । मैं तो आपकी प्रतीक्षा में खड़ी-खड़ी सूखती जा रही हूं । मेरे हृदय में विरह का बाण लग गया है, जिसे मैं एक पल के लिए भी भुला नहीं पाती हूं ।

हे प्रभु! आपने वन में पड़ी हुई अहिल्या का उद्धार कर दिया था । (पति शाप से पत्थर बनी हुई उसे आपने पुनः जीवन दान किया था ।) इस मीरां में ही ऐसा क्या बोझ हैं? मेरे पाप तो सौ की तुलना में पांच सेर अर्थात् नहीं के बराबर हैं । फिर आप मेरा उद्धार क्यों नहीं करते हैं?

Then to palaka ughaado Deenanath

Then to palaka Ughaado Deenanath!
Main hajir-nazir kab kee khadee!

Sajaniyan dushman hoya baithiya,
sabne lagoon kadee!
Tum bin saajan koi nahin hai,
digi naav samanda adee!

Din naheen chain rata nahin nindiya,
sookhoon khadee-khadee!
Baan viraha ka lagya hiye main,
bhooloon na ek ghadee!

Pathar ke to Ahalya taree,
Bana ke beecha padee!
Kahan bojha Meera main kahiye,
sau par eka dharee!

O Lord of distressed! Please open your eyes and look at me. I'm awaiting for your grace-ful glance for a long time now.

My all kith and kin have turned my enemy since I am an anathema to all of them now. O Beloved! None except you appear my own. My tiny life-boat is getting imbalanced and astray in the sea of mundane existence. It is only you who can help it cross it.

I get no relief in days and no sleep during nights. Waiting for your grace I am getting consumed (by my agony of bearing seperation from you) and writhered. My heart is struck with the arrow of love which aches every minute.

O Lord! You had redeemed Ahalya (lying like a stone in the jungle). Is meera so heavy that you can't redeem her? My sins are muchless heavy, in fact lighter than that of her by 20 times*. Why don't you relieve my of my distress.

* The text gives the ratio between the two weights as 100:5 and hence twenty times.

(xxiii)
हरि तुम हरो जन की भीर

हरि तुम हरो जन की भीर

द्रौपदी की लाज राखी
तुम बढ़ायो चीर ।
भक्त कारण रूप नरहरि
धर्यो आप सरीर ।

हिरनकस्यप मार लोनो
धर्यो नाहिन धीर ।
बूड़त गज ग्राह मार्यो
कियो बाहर नीर ।

दासी मीरां लाल गिरधर
दुःख जहां तहं पीर ।
हरि तुम हरो जन की भीर ।

हे कृष्ण! आप अपने भक्तों के संकटों को दूर कीजिए ।

आपने तो सदैव अपने भक्तों के कष्टों का निवारण किया है । जब दुःशासन ने भरी सभा में द्रौपदी के वस्त्र-हरण का प्रयास किया तो आपने ही उसका चीर बढ़ा कर उसकी लज्जा की रक्षा की थी । भक्त प्रहलाद के कारण आपने नृसिंह का रूप धारण किया और दुष्ट हिरण्यकश्यपु को मार गिराया ।

आपने डूबते हुए हाथी की रक्षा के लिए ग्राह को मारा । वो हाथी को पानी में ले जा रहा था और प्रभु आपने ही गजराज को जल से बाहर किया ।

हे गिरधर गोपाल! यह मीरां भी आपकी दासी है । आप स्वयं जानते हैं कि जहां चोट लगती है, वहां पीड़ा भी होती है । मेरे विरह-दुःख को आप जानते हैं अतः उसे दूर करने का प्रयास कीजिए । हे कृष्ण! आप अपने भक्तों के संकटों को दूर कीजिए।

Hari Tum Haro Jana Kee Bheer

Hari Tum Haro Jana Kee Bheer!

Draupadi kee laaj raakhee
aur badhayo cheer!
Bhakta karana roop narahari
Dharyo ap sareer!

Hiranakasyapa mara leeno
Dharyo nahin dheer!
Boodhati gaja graha maryo
Kiyo baahar neer!

Daasi Meera Lal Giridhara
Dukh jahan tahan peer!
Hari Tum Haro Jana Kee Bheer!

O Lord Hari! You must relieve your devotees of their distress. When Dushasana had tried to disrobe Draupadi in an open court, it was you who enhanced the cloth length to save her honour. To protect your devotee Prahlad, you immediately adopted the form of half-man, half-lion (The Narashima Incarnation) and killed the wicked Hiranyakashyapa.

In order to save the drowning elephant you had killed the crocodile and brought the distressed elephant out of water, to safety.

O Gopal* who mounted the hill, this Meera is your servant. You know well that one gets pain, when one gets hurt [i.e. You know well my agony of seperation from you and hence you must condescend to remove it, O Hari! relieve your devotees of their distress.

---

* Literally the one who tends cows. But 'GO' in sanskrit also means senses, hence Gopal also means the one who is the master of the senses.

(xxiv)
तुम सुनो दयाल म्हारी अरजी

तुम सुनो दयाल म्हारी अरजी ।

भौसागर में बही जात हूं,
काढ़ी तो थारी मरजी ।

यो संसार सगो नहिं कोई,
सांचा सगा रघुवर जी ।

मात-पिता और कुटुम्ब कबीलो
सब मतलब का गरजी ।

मीरां की प्रभु अरजी सुन ल्यो,
चरण लगाओ गिरधर जी ।

हे दयालु प्रभु! आप मेरी प्रार्थना सुन लीजिए ।

मैं इस संसार-सागर में बही जा रही हूं, आपकी मरजी हो तो मुझे इससे बाहर निकाल लीजिए अर्थात् इस संसार-चक्र से मेरा उद्धार कीजिए!

इस संसार में कोई अपना नहीं है । यह संसार नितान्त स्वार्थी है । सब स्वार्थ के साथी हैं । यदि कोई सच्चा सम्बन्धी है तो वह एकमात्र भगवान राम (या कृष्ण) हैं । यहां तो माता-पिता और परिवार-कुटुम्ब के सभी व्यक्ति अपना मतलब ही सिद्ध करने वाले हैं ।

हे प्रभु ! आप मीरां की प्रार्थना सुन लीजिए और इसे अपने चरणों में आश्रय दीजिए ।

Tum Suno Dayal Mharee arajee

Tum Suno Dayal Mharee arajee!

Bhausagar main bahee jata hoon,
kadho to tharee marajee!

Yo sansaara sago nahin koyee
Sancha sagaa Raghuvara jee!

Mata-Pita aur kutumba kabeelo,
Sab matlab ka garajee!

Meera ke prabhu arajee sum lyo
Charana lagao Giridhara jee!

O Kind-hearted Prabhu! Please listen to my prayer now!

I seem to be getting drowned in the sea of mundane existence. Should you so condecend to do, please take me out of this cycle of metempsychosis.

There is no one one's own in this world. This whole world is selfish and everyone serving one's selfish ends. if there is any true relation, it is only Lord Rama (or Krishna*), for all, whether parents or other close relations work only with their selfish designs.

O Lord! Kindly listen to Meera's prayer and provide her shelter at your feet.

---

* Since both Rama and Krishna were Lord Vishnu's incarnation, Meera often makes no distinction between them.

(xxv)
तनक हरि चितवौ म्हारी ओर

तनक हरि चितवौ म्हारी ओर ।

हम चितवन तुम चितवन नाहीं
दिल के बड़े कठोर ।

म्हारी आशा चितवनि तुमरी
और न दूजो दोर ।

तुमसे हम कूं तो तुम ही हो
हम सी लाख करोर ।

ऊभी ठाड़ी अरज करत हूं,
अरज करत भयो भोर ।

मीरां के प्रभु हरि अविनासी,
दूंगी प्राण अकोर !

हे कृष्ण! तनिक मेरी ओर अपनी कृपादृष्टि डालिए ।

मैं निरंतर आपकी ओर आशा-भरी दृष्टि से निहारती हूं किंतु आप हमारी ओर देखते ही नहीं हो । निश्चय ही आपका हृद्य अत्यधिक कठोर है ।

हे कृष्ण! आपकी कृपापूर्ण चितवन ही मेरी एकमात्र आशा है । मेरे लिए अन्य कोई ठौर नहीं है ।

हमारे लिए तो आप जैसे बस केवल आप ही हैं परंतु आपको हम जैसे लाखों करोड़ों मिल जाएंगे ।

मैं कब से खड़ी-खड़ी आपसे निवेदन कर रही हूं परंतु आप ध्यान ही नहीं देते । यहां तक कि आपसे दर्शनों की प्रार्थना करते-करते भोर हो गई है ।

हे मीरां के प्रभु अविनासी श्रीकृष्ण, अब तो कृपा कीजिए । मैं आपको अपने प्राणों की भेंट चढ़ाऊँगी अर्थात् आप पर सर्वस्व न्यौछावर कर दूंगी ।

Tanaka hari Chitavo Mharee Or

Tanaka hari Chitavo Mharee Or!

hum chitavat tum chitavat naheen
Dil ke bade kathor!

Mharee aashaa chitavani tumharee
Aur na dooji dor !

Tumse hum koon to tumharee ho
Hum see lakh karor!

oobhee thaadee araj karat hoon
Araj karata bhayo bhor!

meera ke prabhu Hari Avinashi
Doongee praan akor!

O Hari (Krishna) ! kindly shed on me too your gracious sight. While I ever keep on looking wistfully towards you, you seem to never look at me! Certainly your heart is very hard.

O Hari! your graceful look at me is the only hope for me since there is no other place for me to seek succour from! For me you are the unique and only one while for you there could be millions like me!

Since long I stand here and supplicating before you but you never pay any attention to me! So much so, that I pass night praying to you frequently till the dawn [But you never respond].

O Lord of Meera the imperishable Lord Supreme Krishna! Now I will sacrifice my life in this quest. [i.e. I would sacrifice everything that I possess for recieving ought grace from you.]

(xxvi)
जोगी मत जा

जोगी मत जा, मत जा, मत जा ।
पांव परूं मैं तोरे ।

प्रेम भगति कौ पंथ है न्यारो
हमकूं गैल बता जा ।
अगर चंदन की चिता बनाऊँ
अपने हाथ जला जा ।
जोगी मत जा, मत जा, मत जा ।

जल-बल भई भस्म की ढेरी
अपने अंग लगा जा ।
मीरां कहे प्रभु गिरधर नागर
जोत में जोत मिला जा ।
जोगी मत जा, मत जा, मत जा ।

हे योगी! तू मुझे छोड़कर मत जा । मैं तेरे पैर पकड़ती हूं, तू मुझे छोड़कर मत जा, मत जा ।

प्रेम और भक्ति का मार्ग बड़ा निराला और विचित्र है । हे योगी श्रीकृष्ण तुम अपनी प्रेम-योगिनी को वह मार्ग बताओ, जिस पर चलकर यह आपके पास तक पहुंच सके ।

तुम्हारे वियोग में मैं एक क्षण भी जीवित नहीं रह सकती अतः मैं अगरु और चन्दन की चिता बनाऊँगी, इसे तुम अपने हाथों आकर जला जाओ ताकि इस विरहिणी को विरह से मुक्ति प्राप्त हो सके ।

विरह की आग में जलकर मेरा शरीर भस्म (राख) की लौ बन चुका है । तुम इसे अपने अंगों पर लगा लेना ताकि मरने के बाद तुमसे मिलन का सुख प्राप्त कर सकूं । मीरां कहती हैं कि हे गिरधर गोपाल, तुम अपनी ज्योति में मेरी ज्योति को लीन कर लो। तात्पर्य यह है कि मेरी आत्मा तुम्हारा ही अंश है । इसे अपनी ज्योति में लय कर लीजिए ।

Jogee ! Mat Jaa

Jogee! Mat Jaa, mat ja, mat ja!
Panva paroon main tere!

Prem bhagati kau pantha hai nyaro
Hum hoon gail bataa jaa!
Agaru chandan ku chita banaoon
Apne haath jala jaa!
Jogee ! Mat Jaa, mat ja, mat ja!

Jala-bala bhayeen bhasam kee dheree
Apne anga laga jaa!
Meera ke prabhu Giridhara Nagar
Jot mein jot mila jaa!
Jogee! Mat Jaa, mat ja, mat ja!

O Ascetic ! Please I beg and beseech you, falling at your feet-don't go leaving me alone! No doubt the path of love and devotion is strange and extra ordinary. O Ascetic (Shree Krishna) ! You must enlighten your devotee, [that is Me, (Meera) who is madly in love with you] that path which takes her close to you.

[I now can't survive a moment without you and hence] I plan to set a pyre by collecting incense and sandal so that you may come and set it affire with your own hands [with me on it, since I can't live without you.]

In fact burning in the fire of seperation from you this body has virtually become a heap of ash. You may smear this ash upon your body so that I may get this pleasure of being close to you even after my death. O MyLord! who mounted the hill, coalesce my existence with your own divine light! [since it is your part ultimately].

(xxvii)
जोगिया से प्रीत कियां दुःख होइ

जोगिया से प्रीत कियां दुःख होइ ।

प्रीत कियां सुख ना मोरी सजनी
जोगी मित्त न कोई ।

रात-दिवस कल नाहिं परत है
तुम मिलियां बिन मोइ ।

ऐसी सूरत या जग मांही
फेरि न देखी सोइ ।

मीरां के प्रभु कबरे मिलोगे
मिलियां आनन्द होइ ।

हे सखी! निर्मोही जोगिया प्रियतम से प्रेम करने पर दुःख ही होता है ।

उससे प्रेम-सम्बन्ध स्थापित करने पर सुख नहीं मिलता, क्योंकि जोगी किसी का मीत नहीं होता । अर्थात् निर्मोही प्रियतम से प्रेम के निर्वाह की आशा करना व्यर्थ है ।

हे जोगी! तुमसे मिले बिना मुझे रात-दिन एक पल भी चैन नहीं मिल रहा है । आपका रूप इतना अनोखा है कि उस रूप को देख लेने के बाद और कोई रूप आंखों को जमता ही नहीं है ।

मीरां कहती हैं कि प्रियतम! अब तुम कब मिलोगे? तुमसे भेंट करके ही मैं आनन्द को प्राप्त करूंगी ।

Jogia Se Preet Kiyan Dukha Hoya

Jogia se preet kiyan dukha hoya!

Preet kiyan sukh na moree sajani
Jogi mitta na koya!

raat-diwas kala nahin parata hai
Tum miliyan bin moya!

Eisee surat ya jag manhu
Pheri na dekhee soya!

Meera ke prabhu Giridhara Nagar
miliyan ananda hoya!

O Mate ! Loving an emotion-less beloved always causes sarrow. For he is like an eremite. Establishing love with him never brings happiness because an ascetic has no soft corner for any one.

But (despite that I love such a person) I get no relief either for a moment in a day or night. [it is my folly but I can't help since.] Your form is so captivating that once the eyes settle on it they don't want to see any other form.

Says Meera, "O My Beloved! When shall you meet me? It is only by meeting you that I can realise true bliss."

(xxviii)
चलो मन गंगा-जमुना तीर

चलो मन गंगा-जमुना तीर ।

गंगा-जमुना निर्मल पानी
सीतल होत सरीर ।
बंसी बजावत गावत कान्हां
संग लियो बलवीर ।
चलो मन गंगा-जमुना तीर ।

मोर मुकुट पीताम्बर सोहे
कुंडल झलकत हीर ।
मीरां के प्रभु गिरधर नागर
चरन-कमल पै सीर ।
चलो मन गंगा-जमुना तीर ।

मीरांबाई कहती हैं-हे मन! तू गंगा-यमुना के तट पर चल ।

गंगा और यमुना में प्रवाहित होने वाला जल अत्यन्त निर्मल है । उसमें स्नान करने से शरीर के सभी पाप-ताप दूर हो जाते हैं और मन अत्यधिक शीतलता और आनन्द का अनुभव करता है ।

हे मन! तू उस गंगा-यमुना के तट पर चल जहां श्रीकृष्ण ने अपने भाई बलराम को लेकर वंशी-वादन किया था और अपने सखाओं के साथ अनेक प्रकार के गीत गाए थे।

श्रीकृष्ण की सुन्दरता का चित्रण करती हुई मीरां कहती हैं श्री कृष्ण के सिर पर मोर का मुकुट शोभायमान है । वे पीले वस्त्र धारण किए हुए हैं । उनके कानों में कुण्डल सुशोभित हैं, जिनमें हीरे झिलमिला रहे हैं । मीरा कहती हैं कि मेरे प्रभु तो गिरधर नागर श्रीकृष्ण हैं । उन्हीं के चरण-कमलों में मैं अपना मस्तक झुकाए हुए हूं ।

Chalo Mana Ganga-Jamuna teer

Chalo mana Ganga-Jamuna teer!

Gnga-Jamuna nirmal paani
Sheetal hot sareer!
Bansi bajavat gavat Kanha
Sanga liyo Balaveer!
Chalo mana Ganga-Jamuna teer!

Mor-mukut pitambar sohe
Kundal jhalakat heer!
Meera ke prabhu Giridhara Nagar
Charan-kamal pe seer!
Chalo mana Ganga-Jamuna teer

Says Meera Bai: "O mind! Move to the banks of the rivers Ganga-Jamuna!"

The waters of the Ganga and Jamuna are extremely pious which remove all the afflictions and sins of the body. By taking a bath in them, the mind feels delighted and cool.

O Mind! Go to those banks of the holy rivers where Lord Krishna had played flute and with his brother, Balaram, and had frolicked and sang many songs.

These, where Lord had beshone with his head adorned with the crown made of peacock's feathers; he was clad in yellow raiment; his ears decked with comely rings studded with diamonds radiating their glow. Says Meera that her Lord is Shree Krishna, the wise*, who lifted the hill, to whose lotus-feet I ever bow my head.

---

* The actual word used in the text is 'Nagar' which literally means 'urban' but in this context it means the all-knowing Lord.

(xxix)
कोई कहियौ रे प्रभु आवन की

कोई कहियौ रे प्रभु आवन की ।
आवन की मनभावन की ।

आप न आवै, लिख नहिं भेजै
बान पड़ी ललचावन की ।

ए दोइ नैन कह्यो नहिं मानैं
नदियां बहै जैसे सावन की ।

कहा करूं नाहिं बस मेरो
पांख नहीं उड़ जावन की ।

मीरां कहैं प्रभु कबरे मिलोगे
चेरी भई हूं तेरे दावन की ।

कोई तो मेरे स्वामी के आने की बात कहे । मेरे मनभावन प्रियतम से आने का निवेदन करे । मेरे प्रियतम न तो स्वयं आते हैं और न कोई सन्देश भेजते हैं । उन्हें तो मुझे ललचाने (तड़पाने) की आदत-सी पड़ गई है ।

मेरे ये दोनों नेत्र मेरा कहना नहीं मानते, समझाए नहीं समझते । परिणामतः इनसे सावन जैसी नदियां प्रवाहित हो रही हैं (आंखें निरन्तर आंसू बहाती रहती हैं ।)

मैं क्या करूं? मेरा अपने पर वश नहीं रहा है । अतः मैं उड़कर भी आपके पास नहीं आ सकती ।

मीरां कहती हैं कि हे प्रभु! आप कब मिलेंगे? मैं तो आपके दामन की दासी हूं ।

Koyee kahiyo re Prabhu Aawan kee

Koyee kahiyo re Prabhu aawan kee!
Aawan ke manabhawan kee!

Ap na ave, likh nahin bheje
Ban paree lalchavana kee!

Ei doyee naina kahyo nahin mane
Nadiya bahe jaise sawan kee!

Kaha karoon nahi bas mero
Pankha nahin ura jawan kee!

Meera kahe Prabhu kabare miloge
Cheri bhaye hoon tere dawana kee!

Please! Someone must tell me about the arrival of my Lord, my beloved and of the one who has captivated my heart.

My Beloved! Neither you come nor send any message. You seem to be given to teasing all by making false promises.

But my two eyes don't listen to what I tell them and keep on shedding tears uncontrollably like the rains in the month of Sawan that swell and quicken the rivers flow.

What should I do? I seem to have no control over my ownself. I have no wings to fly and reach close to you.

Asks love-lorn Meera, O Lord, when will you meet her? She craves for your protection, [extend it again over me!].

(xxx)
किण संग खेलूं होली

किण संग खेलूं होली,
पिया तज गए हैं अकेली ।
माणिक मोती सब हम छोड़े,
गल में पहनी सेली ।
भोजन भवन भला नहिं लागै,
पिया कारण भई गैली ।
मुझे दूरी क्यों म्हेली ।
अब तुम प्रीति और सो जोड़ी,
हम से करी क्यों पहेली ।
बहु दिन बीते अजहुं न आये,
लग रही तालाबेली ।
किण बिलमाये हेली ।
स्याम बिना जियड़ो मुरझावे,
जैसे जल बिन बेली ।
मीरां को प्रभु दरसण दीज्यो,
जनम-जनम की चेली ।
दरस बिन खड़ी दुहेली ।

मेरे प्रियतम मुझे बिल्कुल अकेला छोड़ कर चले गए हैं। प्रियतम के बिना मैं किसके साथ होली खेलूं?

मैंने अपने सभी मूल्यवान रत्नों को त्याग दिया है और गले में संन्यासियों की माला पहन ली है । अपने प्रिय के वियोग में मुझे न भोजन अच्छा लगता है और न ही भवन सुखकर प्रतीत होता है । अपने प्रियतम के पीछे मैं पागल हो गई हूं । मैं अभी तक इस बात को नहीं समझ पाई कि उन्होंने मुझे अपने से दूर क्यों किया हुआ है?

हमें ऐसा लगता है कि आपने किसी अन्य के साथ प्रेम-सम्बन्ध स्थापित कर लिया है । यदि आपको हमारे साथ ऐसा ही व्यवहार करना था तो पहले हमारे साथ प्रेम का संबंध क्यों स्थापित किया था? अब तो बहुत दिन व्यतीत हो चुके हैं और आप हमारे पास लौट कर नहीं आए हैं। इसी कारण मेरा मन अत्यधिक व्याकुल हो रहा है । न जाने किसने मेरे भोले-भाले प्रियतम को लुभा लिया है?

अपने प्रियतम श्याम के वियोग में मेरा हृदय उसी प्रकार मुरझा रहा है जिस प्रकार पानी के अभाव में बेल मुरझा जाती है । मीरां कहती हैं कि हे प्रभु! मैं आपकी जनम-जनम की दासी हूं, इसलिए मुझे अपने दर्शन दीजिए । आपके दर्शन के बिना मैं अत्यधिक दुःखी और व्यथित हो रही हूं ।

Kin sanga Kheloon Holi

Kin sanga kheloon Holi
Piya taji gaye hain akeli!

Manik moti sab hum chhode
gal main pahani seli!
Bhojan bhawan bhalo nahin lage,
Piya karan bhayee gailee
Mujhe doori kyon mhelee!

Ab tum preeti aur so jodee,
Hum se karee kyon pahelee!
Bahu din beetey ajahoon na aye
Laga rahee talabeli!
Kin bilmaye holi!

Syam bina jiyarho murjhave
Jaise jala bin beli!
Meera ko Prabhu darsan deejyo
Janam-janam kee Cheli!
Daras bin khadi duheli!

Since my beloved has deserted me, who should I play Holi with?

I have now shed wearing all costly gems and have donned around my neck the rosary worn by the ascetics. In my beloved's absence neither I like food nor staying in the palace. I seem to have turned mad in his Love. I still fail to understand as to why has he deserted me?

May be he loves someone else. But if he wanted to stay away from me, why did in the first place he established relation of love with me? Many days elapse and He is still not back. I feel distressed weening someone else arresting him in her love. After all he is quite a simpleton and devoid of any guile. My heart now withers like a creeper without water. O Lord! Meera is your slave for all lives so please come before her. Without seeing you I am immensely grieved and full of sorrow.

(xxxi)
आली म्हांने लागे वृन्दावन नीको

आली म्हांने लागे वृन्दावन नीको ।

घर-घर तुलसी ठाकुर पूजा
दरसन गोविन्दजी को ।
निरमल नीर बहत जमुना में
भोजन दूध दही को ।
आली म्हांने लागे वृन्दावन नीको ।

रतन सिंहासन आप विराजै
मुकुट धर्यों तुलसी को ।
कुंजन-कुंजन फिरत राधिका
सबद सुनत मुरली को ।
आली म्हांने लागे वृन्दावन नीको ।

मीरा के प्रभु गिरधर नागर
भजन बिना नर फीको ।
आली म्हांने लागे वृन्दावन नीको ।

हे सखी! वृन्दावन मुझे बहुत अच्छा लगता है ।

इस वृन्दावन में घर-घर में तुलसीदल द्वारा श्री कृष्ण की पूजा की जाती है । वहां पर श्रीकृष्ण के दर्शन भी सरलता से हो जाते हैं ।

वृन्दावन के अतुलित सौंदर्य का अंकन करते हुए मीरांबाई कह रही हैं कि वृन्दावन में प्रवाहित यमुना का जल अत्यधिक पावन और निर्मल है । भोजन के रूप में वहां दूध-दही पर्याप्त मात्रा में उपलब्ध है ।

हे प्रभु! आप स्वयं तो तुलसी का मुकुट धारण करके रत्न-जड़ित सिंहासन पर विराजमान रहते हो; जबकि आपकी दीवानी राधा आपकी मुरली का सुमधुर स्वर सुनने के लिए एक-एक कुंज में भटकती रहती है ।

प्रेम की आराधिका मीरांबाई कहती हैं कि मेरे प्रभु तो गिरिधर नागर श्रीकृष्ण हैं । उनके गुणकीर्तन के बिना व्यक्ति का जीवन निरर्थक है ।

Aali Mhane Lage Vrindavana Neeko

Aali mhane lage Vrindavana neeko!
Ghar-ghar Tulsi-Thakur pooja
Darshana Govinda jee ko!
Nirmal neera bahat Jamuna main
Bhojana doodha dahi ko!
Aali mhane lage Vrindavana neeko!

Ratan simhasana ap viraje
Mukuta dharyo Tulsi ko
Kunjan-kunjan phirate Radhika
Sabad sunat murali ko!
Aali mhane lage Vrindavana neeko!

Meera ke Prabhu Giridhara Nagar
Bhajan bina nar pheeko
Aali mhane lage Vrindavana neeko!

O mate! I like Vrindavana immensely! In Vrindavana every house worships Shree Krishna by offering Tulsi (leaves) on to the Lord's visage.

Here flows hearby the pious river of Yamuna and peoples' staple diet is curds and milk.

O Lord ! Adorning the crown made of tulasi plant you remain seated on the gem-studded throne while Radha, mad in your love, keeps on wondering every where, in every grove to hear the captivating note of your flute.

Says Meerabai that her Lord is Shree Krishna, who mounted the hill! Without chanting the hymns highlighting the Lord's attributes a person's life is vain and meaningless.

(xxxii)
म्हांरो जनम मरण को साथी

म्हांरो जनम मरण को साथी ।
थांने नहीं बिसरूं दिन राती ।

तुम देख्यां बिन कल न पड़त है, जानत मेरी छाती ।
ऊँची चढ़-चढ़ पंथ निहारूं, रोवं-रोवं अंखिया राती ।

यो संसार सकल जग झूठी, झूंठा कुलरा न्याती ।
दोउ कर जोड़यां अरज करत हूं, सुण लीजो मेरी बाती ।

यो मन मेरी बड़ी कुचाली, ज्यूं मदमातो हाथी ।
सतगुरु हस्त धर्यो सिर उपर, अंकुस दे समझाती ।

पल-पल तेरा रूप निहारूं, निरख-निरख सुख पाती ।
मीरां के प्रभु गिरधर नागर, हरि चरणा चित राती ।

मीरां कहती हैं कि आपका और मेरा सम्बन्ध जन्म-जन्म का है इसलिए मैं आपको किसी भी क्षण, रात-दिन, एक पल के लिए भी विस्मृत नहीं कर सकती ।

आपके दर्शन के बिना मुझे एक क्षण के लिए भी चैन नहीं मिल सकता । यह बात मेरा हृद्य भलीभांति स्वीकार करता है । मैं निरन्तर अपनी ऊँची अटारी पर चढ़ कर आपकी बाट देखती रहती हूं । आपकी प्रतीक्षा में रोते-रोते मेरी आंखें लाल हो गई हैं।

यह संसार असत्य है, छल से भरा हुआ है और इसके सभी सम्बन्ध भी असत्य हैं। परिवार के सदस्यों का पारस्परिक सम्बन्ध भी दिखावामात्र है । मैं आपसे करबद्ध प्रार्थना करती हूं । मेरी इस बात को ध्यानपूर्वक सुन लीजिए ।

मेरा यह मन अत्यधिक दुष्ट प्रकृति का है । यह मदमाते हाथी के समान निरंकुश भी है । मैं अपने मन को वश में करके बार-बार समझाती हूं कि उसे इस प्रकार निरंकुश होकर घूमना शोभा नहीं देता, क्योंकि उसके सिर पर सद्गुरु ने अपनी कृपा का हाथ रखा हुआ है ।

मैं हर पल आपके मनोहारी रूप को निहारती रहती हूं और उस रूप को देख-देख कर सुख का अनुभव करती हूं । मेरे स्वामी तो गिरिधर नागर श्रीकृष्ण हैं । मेरा मन तो उन्हीं के पावन चरणों में अनुरक्त है ।

Mharo Janama-Marana Ko Saathi

Mharo Janama-Marana Ko Saathi!
Thane nahin bisroon din raati!

Tum dekhyan bin kal na padat hai, janata meri chhati!
Oonchi chadh-chadh pantha niharoon, ronv-ronv aakhiyan rati!
Yo sansaar sakal jag jhoothi, jhoontha kulra nyatee!
Dou kara jodiyaan araja karata hoon, sun leejon meri baati!
Yo man mero barho kuchali, jyoon madamato haathi!
Sataguru dasta dharyo sir oopar, ankus de samjhatee!

Pala-pala tera roop niharoon, nirakh-nirakh sukh paati!
Meera ke Prabhu Giridhara Nagar, Hari charan chita rati!

Meera says that since mine and yours relationship spreads to many lives, I just can't forget you even for a moment.

Without seeing you I don't get relief even for a second. This is the fact that my heart confesses. All the time I climb to the top of the house and wait for you. Waiting all the time and crying have made my eyes red with pain.

This whole world is an illusion and deceitful and hence its all relations are untrue. Mutual affection among the members of the family is just sham. Now I pray you handbound! Please listen to my prayer attentively. My mind is by nature wicked and unsteady like an ebriate elephant. I repeatedly try to control it and impress upon it that it doesn't behove it to wander so uncontrollably, particularly when the noble guru is keeping his gracious hand upon it for guidance.

Every moment I keep concentrating on your captivating form and derive pleasure from this vision. My Lord is noble Shree Krishna, the one who mounted the hill (of goverdhana). My mind is ever captivated by those pious feet.

(xxxiii)
राम नाम जप लीजै प्रानी

राम नाम जप लीजै प्रानी
कोटिक पाप कटै रे ।

जनम जनम के खत जु पुराने
नामहिं लेत फठे रे ।

कनक कटोरे इम्रत भरियौ
पीवत कौन नटै रे ।

मीरां कहै प्रभु हरि अविनासी,
तन मन ताहि पटै रे ।

हे प्राणी! तू राम का ही स्मरण कर । राम-नाम का स्मरण करने से तेरे करोड़ो पाप भी समाप्त हो जाएंगे ।

बहुत दिनों से तुम्हारे खाते में (जन्म-जन्मान्तरों से तुम्हारे नाम) जो पापों का हिसाब-किताब लिखा हुआ है, राम का नाम लेते ही वे सभी खाते स्वयं फट जाते हैं ।

मीरां कहती हैं कि प्रभु सोने के प्याले में अमृत लिए बैठा है । वह कौन मूर्ख प्राणी होगा जो उस अमृत का पान करने से इनकार कर दे ।

मीरां कहती हैं कि मुझे जब से अविनाशी ईश्वर प्राप्त हुआ है तब से मेरा तन, मन, आत्मा सब एक हो गए हैं । मेरे मन का द्वन्द्व समाप्त हो गया है । वे जो खंड-खंड मेरे भीतर थे वे समाप्त हो गए हैं । मैं अखंड हो गई हूं ।

Rama Nama Japa leejey, Prani

Rama nama japa leejey, Prani!
Kotik paap katii re!

Janam-janam ke khat ju purane
Namahin leta phatei re!

Kanaka katore imrat bhariye
peevat kaun natei re!

Meera kahe Prabhu Hari Avinasi
Tan-mana taahi patei re!

O Being! Remember only Rama, the mere rememberance of whose name will destroy millions of your sins.

The pages of your account giving the details of your many lives will automatically tear away the moment you chant Rama's name. Meera says that Lord awaits you with a gold vessel filled with nector! [Meaning, you are a stupid if you don't accept the gift.]

Says Meera that ever since she recieved the grace of Imperishable Lord, her body-consciousness, mind and soul have coalesced into one entity. Now all the delimma of her mind has vanished. All the broken bits of her conciousness have united to become a solid whole. Now I am one and imperishable in my existence.

(xxxiv)
राम नाम रस पीजै

राम नाम रस पीजै मनुआ,
राम नाम रस पीजै ।

तज कुसंग सतसंग बैठि नित
हरि चरचा सुण लीजै ।

काम, क्रोध, मद, मोह लोभ कूं,
चित्त से बहाय दीजै ।

मीरां के प्रभु गिरधर नागर,
ताहि के रंग में भीजै ।

हे मन! राम नाम के रस का पान कर । तू राम के नाम का रस-पान कर । (यहां राम का अभिप्राय है जिसमें मन रम गया । मीरां के लिए इसका अर्थ श्रीकृष्ण ही है ।)

हे मन! तू कुसंग का परित्याग कर अर्थात् दुष्ट प्रकृति के व्यक्तियों का साथ छोड़ दे और नित्यप्रति साधु-सन्तों की संगति कर । तू वहां बैठ जहां प्रभु का गुण-गान सुनने को मिले ।

मेरा सुझाव है कि पंच विकारों अर्थात् काम, क्रोध, मद, मोह और लोभ से अपने चित्त को दूर करने का प्रयास करो ।

मीरां कहती हैं कि हमारे प्रभु तो गिरिधर नागर श्रीकृष्ण हैं । हमें उन्हीं के रंग में अपने आप को लीन (निमग्न) कर देना चाहिए ।

Rama-nama Rasa peejey

Rama-nama rasa peejey, Mannua
Rama-nama rasa peejey!

Taji kusanga satasanga baithi nita
Hari charcha suna leejey!

Kaam-krodha, mada, moha lobha koon
Chitta sey bahaya deejey!

Meera ke Prabhu Giridhara Nagar
Tahi ke rang main bheejey!

O Mind! Imbibe the elixir produced by the holy name of Rama [Rama here means one with which the whole sense is instinct, and hence in Meera's context it is Krishna].

O mind! Shun the evil company and seek the association with holymen and sages so that you may listen to the fair glories of the Lord! Shed Lust, anger, arrogance, infatuation and greed, make effort to remove them for your conciousness and become clean.

Says Meera that her Lord is noble Krishna who lifted the mount and her intention is to coaleses her existence with that of her Lord!

(xxxv)
सइयां, तुम बिणि नींद न आवै हो

सइयां, तुम बिणि नींद न आवै हो ।

पलक-पलक मोहि जुग से बीतें, छिनि-छिनि विरह जरावै हो ।
प्रीतम बिणि तिमि जाइ न सजनी, दीपक भवन न भावै हो ।

फूलन सेज सूल होइ लागी, जागत रेणि बिहावै हो ।
कासूं कहूं कुण मान मेरी, कहयां न को पतियावै हो ।

प्रीतम-पंनग डस्यो कर मेरौ, लहरि-लहरि जिव जावै हो ।

दादर मोर पपइया बोले, कोइल सबद सुणावै हो ।
उमगि घटा घन ऊलरि आई, बीजू चमक डरावै हो ।

है कोइ जग में राम सनेहो, ऐ उरि साल मिटावै हो ।
मीरां के प्रभु हरि अविनासी, नैणां देख्यां भावै हो ।

हे स्वामी! मुझे तुम्हारे बिना नींद नहीं आती ।

तुम्हारे वियोग का एक-एक पल मेरे लिए एक-एक युग के समान व्यतीत हो रहा है । प्रत्येक क्षण वियोग की आग मुझे जलाती रहती है । हे सखी! प्रियतम के बिना मेरे भवन का अन्धकार दूर नहीं होता और मुझे प्रकाश के लिए भवन में दीपक जलाना भी अच्छा नहीं लगता ।

श्याम के विरह में फूलों की शैया भी शूलों सी कष्टदायी प्रतीत होती है । सारी रात जागते हुए बितती है । मैं अपनी व्यथा किससे कहूं? मेरी बात कौन मानेगा? कहने से कोई विश्वास भी तो नहीं करेगा ।

प्रियतम रूपी सर्प ने मेरे हाथ में डंस लिया है, जिससे विष लहरा-लहरा कर शरीर में फैल गया है । अब मेरे प्राण निकलने ही वाले हैं ।

(इधर पावस ऋतु आ गई है) दादुर, मोर, पपीहा बोलने लगे हैं । कोयल मधुर शब्द सुना रही है । आकाश में बादलों की घटाएँ उमड़-उमड़कर झुक आई हैं। उनमें चमकती बिजलियां अपनी चमक से भयभीत कर रही हैं ।

क्या संसार में कोई ऐसा भक्त है जो मेरे हृद्‌य की पीड़ा को दूर करे । मीरां कहती हैं कि हे अविनाशी प्रभु! मेरी आंखें आपकी रूप माधुरी को निरन्तर देखते रहना चाहती हैं ।

Saiyyiyaan, Tum bin neenda na aave ho

Saiyyiyaan, tum bin neenda na aave ho
Palaka-palaka mohi jag se beeten
Chhin-chhin virah jaravei ho!
Preetam bina timi jaya na sajani,
Deepak bhawan na bhave ho!
Phoolan sej soola hoi lagee
Jagati raini bihavei ho!
kaasoon kahoon kuna mana mero
Kahyan na ko patiyabe ho!
Preetam-pannag dasyo kar mero
Lahari-lahari jiva jave ho!
Dadar mor papahya bole
Koel sabad sunave ho!
Umagi ghata ghana oolani aayee
Beeju chamaka darave ho.
Hai koi jag meinRam sanehi
Ei ura saal mitave ho!
Meera ke prabhu Hari Avinasi
Naina dekhyan bhave ho!

O My Lord! Your absence doesn't let me sleep for a moment. Each moment of seperation from your passes like an eon with fire of love consuming me. O Mate! Without my beloved the darkness of my house won't vanished; hence my not liking even lighting a lamp.

In seperation from my Lord my bed of roses hurts as though it be full of thornes. Whole night I keep awake, who should I disclose my agony to who would appreciate it or even believe it. (Meanwhile) Sweet rainy season is on with the being like peacock and papiha are welcoming it. Thundering clouds have gathered with frequent flash of lighting frightening me. The seperation from the beloved has stung me like a poisonous snake; toxic sting is spreading all over my body and I'm about to die. Is there anyone in the world who could relieve me of my distress. My Lord! Imperishable, my eyes now long to see you only.

(xxxvi)
हेरी मैं तो प्रेम दिवानी

हेरी मैं तो प्रेम दिवानी, मेरो दरद न जाने कोई ।

सूली ऊपर सेज हमारी, किस विध सोना होय ।

गगन मंडल पै सेज पिया की, किस बिध मिलना होय ।

घायल की गति घायल जाने, की जिन लागी होय ।

जौहरी की गति जौहरी जाने, की जिन जौहर होय ।

दरद की मारी वन-वन डोलूं, बैद मिला नहिं कोय ।

मीरां की प्रभु पीर मिटैगी, जब बैद सांवलिया होय ।

मीरांबाई कहती हैं कि मैं तो गिरिधर गोपाल श्री कृष्ण के प्रेम की दीवानी हूं । इस दीवानेपन के दर्द को मेरे अतिरिक्त कोई नहीं जानता ।

मेरी शैया (सांसारिक वासनाओं के) कष्टों से भरी हुई है । सांसारिक वासनाओं के रहते हुए किस प्रकार चैन की नींद आ सकती है?

मेरे प्रियतम की सेज (शैया) तो आकाश में है । किस मार्ग से पहुंचा जाए? जब मार्ग का पता नहीं है तो मिलन भी संभव नहीं है ।

प्रेम की पीड़ा का अनुभव वही कर सकता है जो स्वयं प्रेम की पीड़ा से पीड़ित हो अथवा जिसने वह पीड़ा दी हो ।

रत्न का मूल्य जौहरी ही जानता है अथवा वह जिसके पास रत्न हो । प्रेम की पीड़ा से व्यथित होकर मैं वन-वन डोल रही हूं, परन्तु इसका उपचार करने वाला वैद्य मुझे कोई नहीं मिला ।

मीरां की यह प्रेम-पीर तो तभी मिटेगी जब सांवलिया स्वयं वैद्य बनकर आएंगे ।

Heyri! Main to prem diwani

Heyri! main to prem diwani,
Mera darad na jane koi!
sooli oopar sej hamaree,
Kis vidhi sona hoi!
Gagan mandal pe sej piya kee
Kis vidhi milana hoi!
Ghayal kee gati ghayal jane,
Ki jin lagee hoi!
Jauharee kee gati jauharee jane
Ki jin jauhar hoi!
Darada kee maree van-van doloon,
Vaid mila nahin koi!
Meera ke Prabhu peer miteigee
Jab vaid sanwaliya hoi!

Says Meerabai that "I am mad in love of Giridhara Gopal [Shree Krishna] and no one can relieve my agony except my ownself."

My bed is replete with the troubles (of worldly affections). How can one sleep amidst so many of worldly temptations and allurements.

But the bed of my beloved is in the sky and which is the way to reach there? When the way is not known how can meeting be ever possible with my beloved? The agony of my love is realisable by either only that one who has suffered it or the one who causes it. The value of a gem is known only to the jeweller or to that one who owns that gem!

Suffering from the agony of love I'm roaming about the jungles and forests but I am yet to meet someone who could treat it. Now the agony will vanish only when my beloved sanwalia (Krishna) comes to me as the physician.